TALES OF SOMERSET STEAM

ROGER EVANS

COUNTRYSIDE BOOKS
NEWBURY BERKSHIRE

First published 2010
© Roger Evans 2010

COUNTRYSIDE BOOKS
3 Catherine Road
Newbury, Berkshire

To view our complete range of books,
please visit us at
www.countrysidebooks.co.uk

ISBN 978 1 84674 170 8

Designed by Peter Davies, Nautilus Design
Produced through MRM Associates Ltd., Reading
Printed by Information Press

Contents

👉

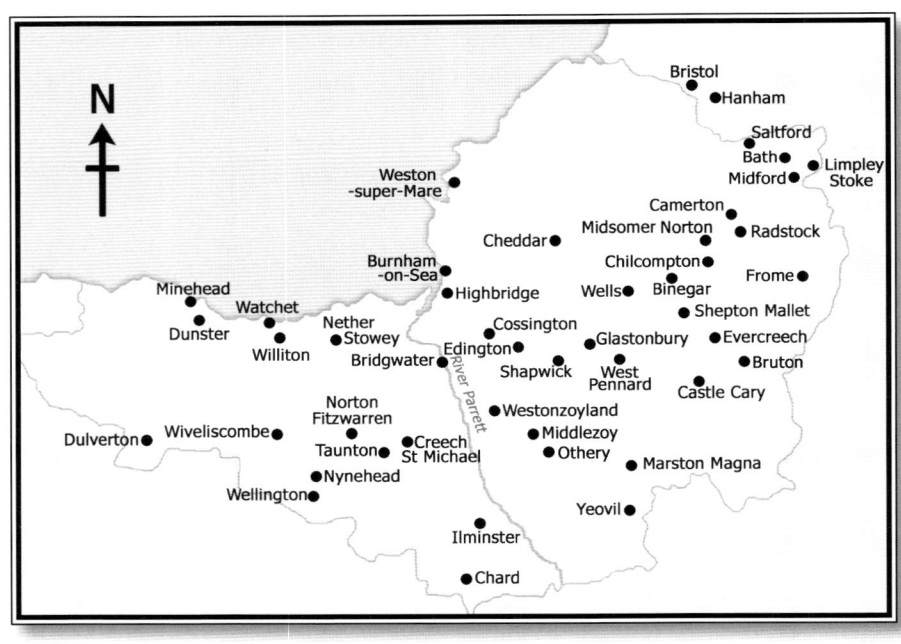

N

Bristol
●Hanham

Saltford
●
Bath●
Weston   Camerton   Midford● ●Limley
-super-Mare●   ●   Stoke

                          Cheddar●   Midsomer Norton● ●Radstock
Burnham   Chilcompton●
-on-Sea●   Wells● Binegar●   Frome●
Minehead   ●Highbridge   ●Shepton Mallet
●   Watchet●   Cossington●   ●Evercreech
Dunster●   Nether●   Glastonbury●
●   Stowey   Edington●   ●Bruton
Williton● Bridgwater●   ● Shapwick● West
                              Pennard Castle Cary
Norton   ●Westonzoyland
Fitzwarren●   Middlezoy
Dulverton● Wiveliscombe●   Taunton● Creech●   Othery● ●Marston Magna
                    ●St Michael
                Nynehead●   Yeovil●
Wellington●
                    ●
                Ilminster

                    ●Chard

River Parrett

6

Introduction

'Steam' — the very word conjures up images of smoke-billowing trains powering across open countryside, leaving their white vapour trails slowly evaporating in their wake. It refreshes memories of seaside trips, buckets and spades, sand in the sandwiches and train-spotting children. It's the stuff of which nostalgia is born and has been the inspiration for crime novels and children's tales from *Murder on the Orient Express* to *Thomas the Tank Engine*. As a theme, there are possibly more Somerset books written about the days of the steam railways than any other single topic, and understandably so when we consider the Somerset & Dorset Railway, the Great Western, the West Somerset Mineral Railway, the Cheddar line and many others. Is it any wonder that when a train exceeded 100 mph for the first time, breaking the world land-speed record, it happened in Somerset?

But steam was more than just about the railways. It heralded the birth of an industrial revolution, when water-driven mills gave way to steam, when mines went deeper thanks to steam-driven water pumps, well before the arrival of the first trains in Somerset. Later it impacted on agriculture and the craft industries in which the county specialised. And more important than these was the impact on the people themselves, from the tragedy of rail disasters to the pleasures of life along the tracks.

That's where I turn my focus: to Somerset folk and the effect steam had on their lives; to people like Reg Travers, to whom this publication is dedicated, a Great Western engine driver of whom I have fond memories, having married his granddaughter; to characters like Martha Vicarey who, having experienced just one journey by rail, swore she'd never ride one again – ''Twas the work of the devil himself'! Read on to discover why.

Roger Evans

Acknowledgements

I would like to acknowledge the following, who were so helpful during my research for this publication:
Keith Barrett; Brian Buttle; Ian Coleby; Dave Fry; Jack Furze; Steve George; Brian Mitchell; David Wright; Somerset County Archives; The Railways Archive.

'TWAS THE WORK OF THE DEVIL HIMSELF

Martha **Vicarey** was a middle-aged farm worker who, in the 1840s, travelled from her Ilminster home to Bridgwater, visiting her daughter, Maria. Martha, accustomed only to horse-drawn travel, had given no thought to what was involved in the second leg of her trip, when she would be travelling by train and pulled by a steam-driven engine.

Martha was accustomed to rising early, her normal working day being from 6 am to 9 pm. She was described as tall and massive of frame without an ounce of superfluous flesh, a body honed by long days of agricultural labouring. On the day concerned, she rose at four, cleaned the house and put on her Sunday best and bonnet, the one she had worn many years before on her wedding day. Having counted out her money, she headed for the Swan Hotel, where she met an acquaintance, a Miss Derby, and asked her if she was going to Taunton. Indeed she was and there would be room for Martha, and the pair departed when the 6 o'clock stage arrived, just as the church clock confirmed the hour.

It was a fine morning with the early dew glistening and birds singing. Martha admired the scenery from her seat perched high up on the coach. Reaching an uphill stretch, she was one of those required to walk, making the load easier for the horses. At the end of five hours, they arrived at Taunton and Martha asked Miss Derby how much her fare would be. A shilling, she was told, and she promptly paid the required amount. That was the common practice; the fare was paid only on the safe arrival. It was eminently sensible – what's the point of paying if you never get there?

Now Martha had been told of 'the train' and how it would take her on to Bridgwater. Miss Derby, recognising Martha's confusion as to where to go, escorted her to the station and explained that she should go inside and

'Twas the Work of the Devil Himself

make her way to the train. Martha stood and looked at the building and could only wonder at how closely it resembled the gaol at Ilchester. Feeling even less confident, she entered the station, looking totally bemused. Help was soon at hand as a friendly member of the station staff enquired. 'Hullo Mother. Where be you a gwaine to?' 'You gurt impudent feller you, said Martha, 'a mothering I. I beant yer mother ner shudden like ta be. I be gwain ta Birdgwater to zee me daater Merier [daughter Maria].' It was an uncalled for retort but the man remained helpful, advising Martha that she should keep an eye on the ticket office window, where she could ask for a ticket once the little door popped up. 'Ticket!' exclaimed Martha. 'I don't want narry [any] ticket.'

Now consider poor Martha in her confused state. She wants to travel to Bridgwater and expects to pay when she arrives. And here is this impudent fellow asking her to pay one shilling and sixpence for a little scrap of paper for which she can see no purpose, not being able to read or write. Convinced they were trying to swindle her, she was even more abusive to the other helpful staff. Then her first helper took control, taking her firmly by both shoulders, giving her a shake, shouting at her and telling her to take the ticket and pay for it. Having been bullied into the payment, she accepted the ticket reluctantly and was escorted to the platform as her helper told her to hurry up or miss the train.

There alongside the platform she saw a long line of carriages, all hitched up, one to the other, unlike anything she'd seen before; one stagecoach after another and not a horse in sight. Looking hard at her helper she enquired in an angry tone, 'What's ee want ta gally [bully] I like this fur? Hassen got the hosses put to eet! [You haven't got the horses put to it yet!]' With the same, the carriage door was opened and Martha was deposited inside a compartment; the ticket was shoved into her hat, with Martha still protesting she didn't want any slip of paper. Looking around, Martha saw, in the opposite corner of the carriage, a large-framed farmer. At just that moment, Martha heard what she took to be a terrifying scream – the train whistle – and was so frightened that the farmer laughed out loud at her situation. 'All right, missus,' he said. 'Look out o winder [window].' Martha did and was shocked to see the world disappearing away from her, the trees and the hedges suddenly moving and the sheep, cows and horses running away so fast that she was sure the end of the world was upon her. She fell to her knees and prayed, reflecting on all her sins and weaknesses, preparing to meet her maker.

'All right, missus. Doant ee be vrightened. Look up,' said the farmer a short while later, knowing that they were just pulling into Bridgwater station. 'Git up an look out an zee where ee be a coming too.' Martha looked out the window, declaring that all she wanted to do was to visit her daughter and she never thought it would 'come to all this'. Then she saw Bridgwater and was even more surprised. How could she possibly be in Bridgwater ten minutes after she left Taunton, when it had taken five hours to travel from Ilminster to Taunton and that wasn't as far as the second bit of her journey? But there on the platform was her daughter. 'O Merier, o Merier,' she cried in relief. 'Lor Mother, how vrightened you da look.' Martha looked back unbelievingly at the train as it pulled out of the station. She later described its departure to her employer: 'Well measter, I turned around an ood ee [would you] believe it? They there carridges went along agen. Not a hoss aright of em but the devil hisself was a drawing of em – tha vire [fire] an tha smoke comm'ed out ov en and on they went – the Lord knows where. I gie thanks that I was relieved from en. Never no more will I have aught ta do wi they there trains. 'Tis the works of the evil one and no other. They da tell I that 'tis in the Book that the devil shall be looked after a thousand years and sure enough the time is come for en to be.'

True to her words, this was the last time that Martha went on the fire-breathing horror. On her return trip she took a coal boat, travelling up the River Parrett using the tide, a journey that would have taken two or three days; but better that than ever go again by train!

Source: Somerset Record Office, Document DD\X\SFF\1: A description of a journey from Ilminster to Bridgwater made by Martha Vicarey [Vickery]. Written by J Perry, Ilminster in dialect (1855).

CHILDHOOD MEMORIES

SURROUNDED BY STEAM

Martha's introduction to the world of steam had clearly been a traumatic experience. For me, it was quite different. I grew up with steam. I was halfway through writing this book when I realised that in my childhood I was completely surrounded by steam. Even the pace of family life was determined by steam, and yet there was not a railway worker in the family. It needs some explanation. I grew up near the cattle market in Bridgwater, a location that was completely surrounded by the railways. Imagine a triangle drawn on a map using railway lines, each side about half a mile long. The three sides of my triangle were formed by the old Great Western Railway, the Somerset & Dorset and the branch line to the docks. My home was right in the middle of that triangle, surrounded by the sounds, sights and smell of steam.

I remember the years after the war when we were allowed to stay up late on New Year's Eve. On the stroke of midnight, the engines in the two stations and sidings would sound their whistles. From the dock, just half a mile away, we would hear the simultaneous sound of ships' sirens, mingling with the church bells. The ships are long gone and steam has been replaced by diesel, and the magical sounds of New Year's Eve have changed forever.

Our rhythm as a family was, to some extent, dictated by the railways. Father was a postman and worked shifts. In contrast to the workers in the nearby factory, who worked conventional shift times, such as 6 to 2, or 2 to 10, father's shift would start at peculiarly odd times such as 17 minutes past 4 in the morning! It all revolved around the times that the mail train arrived, or the time by which the outgoing mail had to be on the platform. It would never have occurred to us that the mail would one day travel by road and air rather than rail and ship.

As youngsters, we roamed freely in our own part of town and much time was spent on or along the railway line. Life was more relaxed then. We would climb down the embankment, by the Bath Road railway bridge, to a trackside telephone, which we would use to call the man in the nearby signal box or at the station. It just couldn't happen now but, in those childhood days, it seemed the normal thing to do. We'd pick up the phone, turn the handle and wait for a response. Occasionally it would be 'Get off that b****** phone and get off the b****** line or your mother will hear about this', at which point we'd scarper! Or more often than not, we'd have a chat with the man at the other end who probably knew father and he would advise us as to when we could next expect a passing train. A game we used to play was guessing when a train would arrive. There was a technique to this. Long before we could see the trains, we could hear them coming. If you listened to the track, the track would tell you. You would know if it was an up-train or down-train. The up ones were the best to predict. They had to cross the out-of-sight Somerset Bridge over the River Parrett. The pitch of the hum altered as the train crossed the bridge. Even as junior-school-aged youngsters, we could guess the speed from the changing pitch, and from that guess how far we could count before it arrived.

Nearby was a Second World War pill box, a great vantage point for train spotting. None of us were more than 10 years old but somehow we'd scramble on top, well out of harm's way, and wait for the trains. During moments of boredom, we'd place pennies on the line to see how big we could get them to grow, compressed by the weight of the wheels on the passing trains. But it only ever worked once. A penny, having been flattened and widened by the experience, never seemed to grow any further no matter how many more trains went over it.

A one-penny platform ticket entitling the holder to spend an hour on the platform.

It was a waste of penny, which perhaps could have been better spent on a platform ticket. This allowed the holder to spend one hour on the station platform, not really long enough for serious train spotting, so was it any wonder that we spent so many hours on top of the pill box? The ticket had the

The Fry's Five Boys chocolate bar.

numbers 1 to 12 along the two longest edges, and one of these would be clipped to indicate the time of entry. One attraction on the platform was the chocolate vending machine, which none of us could afford to use in those days. It was the Fry's Five Boys chocolate bar, memorable for the five faces, one on each section of the bar, showing the same face changing from sad to smiling. It also struck me as oddly unfair that there were two waiting rooms on each platform. One was for anybody but the other strictly for ladies only.

Another childhood mystery was what happened to second class rail travel. I can only remember first class and third class; albeit, for the privileged few, it was possible to obtain a first class ticket at a reduced price! For a shilling, a third class seat could be reserved. Even prams and bicycles required their own tickets.

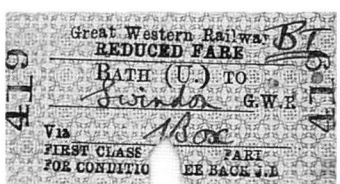

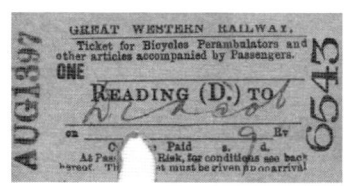

GWR third class, reduced first class, reservation and bicycle tickets.

TALES OF SOMERSET STEAM

RIDES ON THE FOOTPLATE

Just yards down the road, heading towards the town centre, the Great Western branch line to the docks crossed the main road at the point where the A38 and A39 join at what is known as the Cannon junction, or the Cross Rifles roundabout, depending to which generation you belong. The road was far too wide to have a gate here, so the only safe arrangement was for a railway employee to walk in front of the train carrying and waving two red flags. If this conjures up images of the pioneering days of steam, then trust me, it was still happening into the 1960s.

It was a little shunter that crossed the road well before health and safety 'madness' took control. It may not have been in the train driver's rule book, but nonetheless, once in a while, he would help us onto the footplate and we'd be given a ride over to the docks. She was a little bit special, that engine, shunter number 1338. Because we were allowed on her footplate, she became important to us – our little engine.

Engine 1338, which served Bridgwater Docks, now looking very smart again after restoration.

She was one of a class of only two tank engines built for the Cardiff Railway in 1898. When the Cardiff Railway was absorbed into the Great Western in 1923 she was given the number 1338. Her sister engine, 1339, was cut up in 1934 but 1338 survived and did wartime service in Swansea after which she was transferred to the Taunton depot to serve the docks at Bridgwater. Her Somerset days came to an end in 1960 when she returned for a further stint in Swansea.

There she remained in service until 1963, able to boast that she was the last surviving Great Western engine still in operation, having completed an incredible 354,000 miles – and she was only a little thing. She thoroughly deserved to be rescued in 1964 from the scrapheap, and was moved back to Somerset where she rested up at the Bleadon and Uphill station. There she remained in hiding behind an ever-expanding hedge until in 1987 she was moved to Didcot to be restored to full working order.

In 2000 I was one of a small team that organised a series of celebrations, honouring the 800th anniversary of my home town of Bridgwater. We wanted to arrange a number of events that would remind the townsfolk of the heritage of our town. As part of those celebrations, one of our small band, Brian Buttle, a railway enthusiast, arranged for 1338 to make a return trip to Somerset. The surprising aspect of this venture was the cost. Although she had been fully restored and certified, it was cheaper to have her delivered by road than to have her arrive by rail! But come she did and she was displayed in the grounds of Bridgwater College, proving herself to be one of the highlights of the day. It was grand to stand and stare, reflecting on my days as a young schoolboy, riding on her footplate.

SUNDAY SCHOOL OUTINGS

Perhaps my most memorable railway activity – associated with the Somerset & Dorset line – was our annual Sunday school outings. My mother was a pianist at the local Methodist church and was also involved in the afternoon Sunday school. Needless to say, I was obliged to attend each week, but one benefit of attendance was that it qualified you for the annual train ride to Burnham-on-Sea. We would all meet up at the church hall, complete with our packed lunches, buckets and spades, from where we would march crocodile-fashion to the Bridgwater North station.

The last leg – approaching Bridgwater North station on the S&D line, circa 1952.

Someone on the organising committee must have taken tide times into consideration because the tide was always in, but the weather was less predictable. In rainy weather, we would all take shelter under the pier. There was a tea room, which was patronised by the adults whilst we played on the sands until the call came for the journey home. Tired and weary, we made our way back to the nearby station and waited for the following year to come around.

It was a rare treat and in stark contrast to today's expectations of foreign travel. The nine-mile trip to Burnham was a major experience and one not to be missed. I was somewhat taken aback by the actions of an old friend who showed no allegiance to any church but would always attend the Monmouth Street Methodist Sunday school ten times a year, and likewise the King

Street Methodist church. Why ten? That was the number of attendances required to qualify for the Sunday school outing. He got two trips a year. I was once talking to Don Templeman, an old friend of my father, about this very point. Don, who was about 40 years older than me, remembered that he also used to go with the Monmouth Street Methodists and, to prove his point, he produced an attendance card that he had kept from around 1913. On examining the card, I pointed out that it was actually a Baptist Church card. Don said, 'Yes, that's right. I went with the Baptists, Monmouth Street Methodists, King Street Methodists and the Mariners' Chapel'! And sure enough, on his card were ten attendance stars, no more, no less.

A GWR poster promoting travel to Somerset.

How remiss of me, spending all of this time reflecting nostalgically on my youth, when I should have been delving back even deeper into the past to explore the early days of steam in the county, well before the railways arrived.

3

STEAM REACHES SOMERSET

SOMERSET COALFIELDS

Ask the question 'When did steam first arrive in Somerset?' and, unless you're an industrial archaeologist, the instinctive response is to think about the arrival of the Great Western Railway, but a steam-driven engine had arrived almost a century before. Its potential had already been recognised in the industrial Midlands and its arrival in Somerset in 1745 was thanks to the need to take the North Somerset coal mines to even greater depths. Coal had lain beneath the coalfields of North Somerset for millions of years and for centuries it had been known that the seams of coal ran obliquely beneath the surface, reaching deeper and deeper. During the early 17th century, mining took place where these seams broke the surface. They were excavated initially by tunnelling and then by driving shafts vertically downwards to reach the seam, and from there excavating laterally. Ladders were fixed to the sides of the shafts so that the miners could climb down to their place of work, with the baskets of coal being hauled up by ropes, using manpower and later on horse-power.

By the middle of the 18th century, the way that coal seams worked was well understood and the mines were going deeper. Shafts were lined with bricks and air-vents sunk in strategic places. The main barrier to deeper mining was the impracticality and high cost of pumping the mines to keep them dry. And so, in 1745, the Newcomen pumping engine was installed at Paulton's Engine Colliery to pump out the water. His engine design was to dominate the world of pumping for decades to come. In 1780 Jonathan Hornblower erected a compound pumping engine at Middle Pit, Radstock. But still the coal was hauled manually. It was not until 1794 at Radstock's Old Pit that steam-driven winding engines were introduced. The coalfields were by now established as the most significant employer in North Somerset, thanks to steam, and survived until 1973.

STEAM IN THE MILLS

The industrial woollen and silk mills in Somerset had, in the main, been water-powered and hence their presence where fast-running water could be relied upon in towns such as Frome and Bruton. With steam power taking off in the Midlands, Somerset had to catch up to remain competitive. James Hoddinott of Witham Friary was the first to introduce it into his Albion or Milton Silk Mill just outside Evercreech. Three years later Frome's South Parade Mill joined the throng, followed by the Adderwell woollen mill in 1810. By the 1820s steam was well established in the North Somerset mines and textile mills, but still had to penetrate elsewhere. In 1827 a Boulton and Watt beam engine was installed on the Bridgwater and Taunton Canal. At the same time, William Ashman introduced Somerset's first steam-driven railway locomotive on the Somerset Coal Canal's tram-road to Midford, almost half a century after steam's arrival in the coal mines. The first passenger steam loco had to wait another 14 years, pending the arrival of the Bristol & Exeter Railway company.

STEAM COMES TO FARMING

In the mid-19th century the world of agriculture was slipping into a deep depression. A succession of poor harvests combined with cheap imports had driven the farming community to the brink of ruin. The arrival of the railways, especially for the Somerset farming community, had been a real boon. Milk could now reach the large towns and cities whilst still fresh. Cheddar cheese could travel further afield into the nation's urban markets. This had protected local agriculture against the worst effects of the depression, but the time was right for another farming revolution and steam provided the catalyst.

Steam-driven threshing machines and chaff cutters were introduced, replacing the time-consuming manual methods. Needless to say there was an impact on the farm labourers who were no longer in such demand. So the introduction of steam was not popular in all quarters and the vicar of Nynehead, from his pulpit, strongly censured the owner of a local large estate referring to his 'horrible engines cultivating his great fields, smoking and whistling and puffing'.

Steam's greatest impact on Somerset farming was its ability to pump away floodwater from the Somerset Levels. The first major scheme came on the Northmoor. In Norfolk, windmills had already been used for years. In Somerset, steam was preferred. In 1830 an Act of Parliament allowed for the enclosure and drainage of land around Othery, Middlezoy and Westonzoyland. From this was born the Westonzoyland pumping station and it is to the credit of those with vision that this station, the first of its kind, has been restored and maintained by a preservation society, the Westonzoyland Engine Trust. Its scoop wheel, powered by a 27-horse-power engine, was found to be inadequate to drain 1,600 acres of moorland. So in 1861, the 1830 pumping engine was complemented with the addition of an Easton and Amos drainage machine, which stayed in service right through to 1951. This has subsequently been restored and is today driven by steam. After 1861, these engines were replicated across the Somerset Levels, increasing agricultural productivity whilst the advent of the railways increased the size of the market for the Somerset farmers.

4

THE RAILWAY ARRIVES

BRUNEL'S INFLUENCE

In 1833 the Great Western Railway Company appointed a young 26-year-old chief engineer, Isambard Kingdom Brunel. He was to become a legend, cutting tunnels through high ground, taking bridges across rivers, and driving the railways deep into Wales and the West Country. The GWR's railway link from London reached Bristol, passing through Bath on its way and thus creating Somerset's first stretch of passenger railway as it crossed the county boundary five miles east of Bath. It had taken eight years to complete and acted as the catalyst for the creation of the Bristol & Exeter Railway. The funds required to take a line from Bristol, through Bridgwater, Taunton and Wellington, down to Exeter were raised and once again Brunel was employed as the engineer. The railway reached its first destination of Bridgwater on 1st June 1841.

BRIDGWATER CELEBRATES

The official opening had yet to happen but nonetheless, on 1st June, the *Fireball,* towing six carriages and 400 passengers from Bristol Temple Meads, arrived at Bridgwater station. It was a journey that had taken an hour and three quarters for the 32-mile trip. The passengers stopped at Bridgwater long enough for a champagne lunch and returned to Bristol. Almost two weeks later, on 14th June, the official opening took place with the band of the West Somerset Yeomanry, Bridgwater's own regiment, providing the musical entertainment. To the horror of the locals, the official name-plate for the BRIDGWATER station was unveiled and had been misspelt 'BRIDGEWATER', with the extra 'E'. Further embarrassment followed as it dawned on those responsible that scores of newly-placed milestones perpetuated the error.

One of many misspelt milestones.

The impact of the railway was immediate. At the time of its arrival, the town extended no further than the end of Eastover at one end of the town and the Malt Shovel Inn at the other. In the wake of the arrival of the railway, long lines of hundreds of terraced houses sprang up in the vicinity of the station.

It now made sense for the main stagecoach pick-up point to be at the railway station instead of the town centre. At this early stage in the development of the railway, the line only reached down as far as Bridgwater. The station did have, however, an up line and a down line. When a train arrived from Bristol, it would offload its passengers onto the down platform and then shunt the short distance beyond the station to a point where the train could cross from one line to the other. Hence there was a short section of track which, although going nowhere, ran beyond the end of the station platform. It was natural for the stagecoaches visiting the station to turn around in this otherwise unused space. One of these was the *Exquisite,* the Exeter stagecoach, whose driver was so accustomed to turning his coach in this area that, when an engine driver decided to manoeuvre from one line to the next, the belligerent coach driver decided to turn his coach at the same time. In theory this manoeuvre was controlled by a signalman, but when the train was positioned to change tracks, the engine blocked the signalman's view of the stagecoach, so he signalled the 'clear to move' just as the coach was approaching the crossing. The train driver won the argument, the stagecoach overturned, three passengers were injured including one who received a broken ankle, and the railway engine left the rails. It was a small miracle that the injuries were so few since there were twelve passengers on board.

The worst injury was sustained by a 73-year-old lady who was a persistent loiterer around the station. Shortly before the accident, a porter had warned her to get off the line, for her own safety, and he directed her to a position

The Railway Hotel, Bridgwater, with the local stagecoach service.

The staff at Bridgwater station, 1865.

where she would be out of harm's way. It was the very spot where the coach landed when it turned over, breaking her leg just above the ankle.

LIKE CATTLE TO THE GREAT EXHIBITION

The railway was still a novelty in 1851 when London held the Great Exhibition. It was an event that captured the imagination of the nation, and hundreds of thousands of citizens from home and abroad were to enjoy the experience. When an excursion was organised from Bath to the exhibition, the local interest was overwhelming. Even though the train was not due to leave until 6.30 am, trippers were already queuing by 5.30. By 6 o'clock, the booking hall was crammed full and hundreds were waiting outside, pressing to get in. No previous excursion had exceeded 800 passengers, and that in itself was a huge number, but this trip was to more than double that previous record. It was soon realised that insufficient carriages had been organised.

It must be remembered that, in those days of the mid-19th century, it was normal practice for excursions to be in horse-drawn wagons, open topped. It was a slower pace of life. So perhaps it should come as no surprise that the railway company's solution to the overcrowding problems was to lay on an extra three open-topped goods wagons. By the time the train pulled out, even those were full and the train left with 1,600 passengers and at least 200 disappointed people left stranded at the station. A similar excursion from Bristol carried 1,700 passengers in coaches, and such was the load that the train required three engines to pull it.

A LATE ARRIVAL AT YEOVIL

The townsfolk of Yeovil must have felt they had been waiting for ever when their railway finally arrived. It was October 1853, twelve years after Bridgwater. Yeovil people were prepared to show that it was better late than never and the celebrations were to reflect the importance attached to its arrival. A dinner was organised at the Town Hall but, controversially, the ticket prices were so high that only the wealthy and the gentry could attend, causing much ill feeling.

At 11.30 am a lengthy procession formed up, its members reflecting the civic importance of the occasion. First came the Yeovil Brass Band, then members of the Yeovil Guardian Friendly Society, because they had the biggest banner, then the uniformed Sergeant-at-Mace, the town's portreeve, burgesses, Committee of Management, the Commissioners and various other gentry. They were followed by the representatives of the manufacturers and tradesmen (having closed their businesses for the day), and then anyone else who had a banner. Arriving at the station, there was a short outburst of rain which drove them under cover. Then the cloud disappeared and out they popped again when word came that the first train to arrive at Yeovil had been sighted approaching the station. The band picked up their instruments, formed up in order and prepared to play the welcoming cavalcade. But it was a false alarm. Feeling somewhat foolish, they replaced their instruments and waited. Then came the news that the train really was arriving, and they girded their loins once more – only to realise it was another false alarm. Several times this happened and each time they felt a little more foolish. But the band was not to be beaten and simply struck up with their rendition of 'Oh dear, what can the matter be', bringing laughter all round.

The long-awaited train pulled into the station as the band played 'See the Conquering Hero Comes'. A tumultuous cheer erupted from the thousands assembled on the platform as the directors of the Bristol & Exeter alighted. Thomas Binford, the portreeve, stepped forward: 'Gentlemen, I am happy to see you. I have no robe of office, neither have I a written address, but I brought you that which is far better, thousands of warm hearts and happy faces.' The chairman of the rail company replied: 'You could not have conferred greater compliment on us, or given us a warmer welcome than by bringing the numerous assemblage which we see around us.' The party moved in procession to the Town Hall where the banquet had been laid on. Despite the prohibitive cost, the demand was great and tickets had sold out well in advance. Did they have ticket touts in those days? You bet they did. Tickets ended up selling at double their face value.

Following the arrival of the railway, trade boomed in Yeovil. Goods from the Midlands appeared in shop windows for the first time. Coal, so important to the manufacturing industries, became more cost effective. But it wasn't all about incoming trade. Glove making was just one example of how easier access could boost an industry, with local production increasing by almost 50% in just three years to around five million pairs a year.

Onwards to Minehead and beyond

The Bristol & Exeter's next branch line came in 1862 when the West Somerset Railway was opened to Williton and Watchet, finally reaching Minehead in 1874 and allowing the town to embrace its full potential as a holiday resort. Closed as a result of the Beeching cuts, it has since reopened and continues to operate a number of steam trains along this most scenic of lines. Further branches were opened, to Wiveliscombe and onwards to Barnstaple, to Frome, Castle Cary, Pen Mill at Yeovil, to Radstock (just for the coal trade), to Shepton Mallet and Wells. The Great Western was swallowing up other companies, like the Bristol & Exeter, and the Devon & Somerset Railway, but they weren't having it all their own way. There was competition, in particular from the Somerset & Dorset.

SOMERSET & DORSET RAILWAY

In 1854 the Somerset Central Railway Company opened a line. It was operated by the Bristol & Exeter Railway Company between Highbridge wharf, where coal was brought in from South Wales, and Glastonbury. It was extended to Burnham-on-Sea in 1858 with the vision that ferries would bring passengers across from Wales and they could then travel all the way down to Poole on the Dorset coast. From there, they could take a ship to France. In 1860 the Burnham Tidal Harbour and Railway Company was formed, which boasted a fast steamer service offering both the shortest and cheapest route from South Wales to the South West. At Burnham,

Celebrating the centenary of the Somerset Central Railway in 1954.

the rail track continued past the station right down to the shoreline where a sloping stone pier was built, stretching out into the muddy Parrett estuary.

At the other end, the link was set up to Cherbourg and for a brief spell, between 1865 and 1866, the full 'Wales to France' experience was on offer. The scheme failed when the Severn Tunnel was constructed, offering a much faster alternative, but at least it had provided a line from Burnham to Glastonbury and the opportunity to run branch lines elsewhere. The first was to Wells in 1859 and onwards to Cole, near Bruton, in 1862. Meanwhile similar developments were happening with the Dorset Central Railway and the two companies amalgamated in 1862 to form the famous Somerset &

A GWR excursion ticket from Tondu in South Wales to Weston-super-Mare acknowledges the use of 'Campbell's Steamer'.

Dorset Railway which was later, in 1874, to open up lines to Radstock and Shepton Mallet, with the extension to Bath. It wasn't until 1890 that Bridgwater joined the S&D network when the new line gave the opportunity for day-trippers from Bridgwater to visit Burnham beach via Edington Junction. The terminus at the Bridgwater end was situated where McDonalds and Sainsbury's now have their outlets, and it was from here that many a Sunday school outing provided the annual trip to the seaside.

Midsomer Norton station which also served neighbouring Welton.

FAIRS AND CARNIVALS

An additional benefit of the link that had been created between Bridgwater and Glastonbury was that the townsfolk of Glastonbury were now able to travel with relative ease to Bridgwater for its annual fair at the end of September, and its November Guy Fawkes Carnival celebrations. On bonfire night, across the nation, bonfires would be lit and, in some towns, costumed processions would take place. So popular was this pastime in Glastonbury that in one year they actually had two competing processions. But the real competition came from Bridgwater. It was, and remains, the largest of all the carnivals. With Glastonbury's carnival arrangements in some disarray, when the railway reached the town, people were able to commute to Bridgwater to see that carnival, deserting their own. It was

'The last train to Bridgwater Fair' – from an old postcard.

so nearly the death of Glastonbury's procession but fortunately it survived and today flourishes.

THE GREAT RAILWAY SWINDLE

Although the link to Edington opened in 1890, there had been an earlier attempt in 1875 to open the line, which proved to be a financial scam, when the Bridgwater Railway Company was formed. The argument in favour of a new railway was that nine out of ten trains on the Bristol & Exeter railway ran late! It was argued that it was quicker to get to London by horse and cart than by using the Bristol to Exeter line. How did the scam work? In a nutshell, investors put large sums of money into the scheme, and solicitors took out almost as much in legal fees. The appropriately-named Mr Toogood, the brains behind the scheme, was persuaded by the Bristol & Exeter Railway Company not to pursue the proposal on the basis that it would only result in a price war, with both companies losing. Toogood agreed subject to the Bristol & Exeter paying his expenses – which were enormous. In 1882 Toogood was at it once more. Again, huge sums of money and fat solicitors' fees but this time no bribe from the B&E, and no second railway. Bridgwater had to wait until 1890 for its second line.

The day the new station opened at Bridgwater, with its stationmaster and four porters, it poured down and the celebrations were a washout. However, the company operated profitably and the first decade saw much activity with cattle pens, toilets, stables and platelayers' huts being constructed. A limestone quarry was opened at Cossington, taking advantage of the rail link, and the Bear Creek Oil Company opened a depot at the Bridgwater station. A 400-ft wharf was constructed along the river, on the east bank. By 1892, there were nine trains each way to London and Southampton, offering a practical alternative to the Bristol & Exeter.

THE UNPLANNED COST OF THE RAILWAYS

Building a railway inevitably involved the unexpected incident. Some were tragic, there being scores of deaths during the creation of the railway network. But there were other unexpected complications. In 1840, when the Great Western was cutting the railway near Bath, it was necessary to take the line through the grounds of Twerton Vicarage. The railway company had arranged for an alternative house to be built for the family who lived there. Unfortunately, before they had been able to move, the navvies excavating the line managed to cut through the drains of the house. The result was an outbreak of cholera and the tragic death of the vicar's son. A similar problem occurred later that year when the navvies were working in the vicinity of what would become Saltford station. A tunnel of 176 yards was cut and, in so doing, the navvies appeared to have cut through the spring that supplied fresh water to Saltford village. For the best part of the next ten years, the Great Western Railway Company had to supply Saltford with water delivered by horse and cart. They called it progress!

THE SOCIAL IMPACT OF THE RAILWAY

VICTIMS OF PROGRESS

Mention has already been made about how trade and commerce boomed after the arrival of the railways. Whilst Somerset landowners and manufacturers would hope to sell to such towns and cities as Weston, Bristol and Bath, with the arrival of the railways, the local Somerset papers were suddenly displaying advertisements from wholesalers as far afield as Liverpool, seeking to buy their produce. Businesses of all sizes were to benefit, but there was also an opposite reaction in many areas. Steam-powered mechanisation had driven agricultural workers from the fields into the towns; good news for the farmers but not for the labourers, and this was during a period when the vast majority of the population were agricultural labourers. Life was already hard for the rural communities whose welfare was so dependent on a successful harvest. In a bad year, families could be at the point of starvation, but the arrival of steam was another nail in their coffin. The number of new jobs created in the wake of steam and the railways was nowhere near a match for the number of jobs displaced and huge numbers became unemployed. There was no welfare system as we understand it today; the poor died of malnutrition. A farm labourer could perhaps be forgiven for taking violent action against 'modernisation'. With food prices high, there was political unrest in the county and in 1830 the landlords and farmers for miles around Ilchester took the decision to dismantle their threshing machines for fear that the agricultural labourers would burn them down in an act of vengeance. Where tied cottages were left vacant, the furniture was removed for the same reason.

For the displaced agricultural labourers, their search for employment took them into the towns, but urban levels of unemployment were equally bad and, if work was found, it was low-paid, menial labouring. For those thousands who failed to find employment, the workhouse awaited their arrival. The advent of the railways brought a decline in coastal shipping, coal now arriving by rail from South Wales. It also heralded the fatal decline in canal trade, with the rail routes following the same course as the canals and in direct competition. This caused a second but lesser wave of unemployment on the back of the agricultural revolution. It was perhaps no wonder that Somerset had a higher level of unemployment in the 1840s than any other West Country county.

Whilst the arrival of the steam had caused such high levels of unemployment with no compensating job creation, the arrival of the railway at least provided part of the solution to the problems of its own making, both in terms of offering new employment and in 'disposing' of the unemployed by way of emigration.

THE WORKHOUSES AND EMIGRATION

Each parish had a responsibility to look after its poor, and hence the parishes had their own workhouses. This was an inefficient practice and consequently 17 Poor Law Union Workhouses were introduced across the county covering the needs of combined parishes, for example Bridgwater's Union Workhouse was intended for 40 parishes from as far afield as Shapwick and Nether Stowey. Conditions in these new workhouses were better than the old parish ones but were still diabolical. Each was run by a committee whose goal was to reduce the burden to the taxpayer. There was actually a rule that no one in a workhouse should be fed better than the worst fed labourer. The food allowance was eight ounces of bread a day (six for the ladies) and a pint and a half of gruel. On that inadequate diet, those fit to work would be employed in stone crushing for road maintenance. Conditions were crowded, dirty and terrifying; children six to a bed, adults two to a bed and 50 to a room, nine yards by five. In the winter months of 1837, 41% of the inmates of Bridgwater's workhouse died compared to 3% in the prisons. Life outside the workhouse was also harsh with most agricultural labourers' cottages having earth floors and no ceilings. It was a cold and damp, rheumatism-inducing environment especially in the long, wet, low-lying Somerset winters. Against this background, the prospect of emigration to the New World must have been quite attractive despite the associated risks.

The government was keen to populate the colonies and emigration agents were appointed across the Somerset towns with powers to offer assisted passage overseas for the fit and healthy. All that the emigrant needed to find was a sea-worthy trunk for clothing plus the fare to London or Plymouth, which were the nearest emigration ports. Often the parish would find the money, it being cheaper to 'freight' the problem out of the area rather than continue endlessly providing support. Once the railway arrived in the county, the cost of getting rid of the fit and healthy from the workhouses plummeted and so the railway had provided a much needed solution. Emigration was an attractive proposition.

ALONG MILITARY LINES

In stark contrast, for those who gained employment with the railway companies, it was a uniformed position and a job for life. The railway companies were, on the whole, good employers. Examples are easily found of lack of training for its employees, of long hours leading to tiredness and mistakes, but these have to be taken in the context of working conditions generally at that time. Compared to the lot of the agricultural labourer or mill worker, it was the dream job.

By 1850, across the nation, 60,000 people were employed on the railways. By 1875 this had risen to a quarter of a million, and 600,000 by 1905, just over half of these on operational duties, 200,000 on rolling stock and around 80,000 in ancillary roles such as in the railway hotels, buffet services, docks and canal, and the steamships. There were over 800 different categories of jobs; wheeltappers, lamp men, firemen, fire droppers, gardeners, timekeepers, et cetera. For the ladies, there were such roles as barmaids, laundry workers and telegraph clerks.

With such large numbers, it needed to be and was run like an army, the generals being the engineers such as Brunel. It was more than just the uniform that provided

A GWR pay cheque token.

parallels with military service. Ex-soldiers were favoured for employment, particularly those from the Royal Engineers. The language was military; employees 'reported for duty' and there was an expected loyalty to the uniform as there would be to a regiment. As early as 1840, laws had been introduced that made it a criminal offence to disobey company rules, imprisonment being the punishment.

As with the army, there was a hierarchy and order of progression through the ranks. Life for a young lad would perhaps have started with engine cleaning. It could take ten hours to clean one engine. After a couple of years, he could progress to become a 'passed cleaner' and from that position could, on a temporary basis, serve as a fireman, eventually taking up a permanent fireman role. Serving alongside an experienced driver, he could learn the driving skills and progress to become an 'emergency driver', then a driver on freight and passenger trains, ultimately gaining the highest status as a main-line driver. By this time, he'd be at least ten years older but he would have status, even to the point where at hotels, and even in railway pubs, drivers sat at separate tables to the lower ranks.

Within such a large organisation, there was inevitably an 'us and them' atmosphere, with those who worked on the track (drivers, firemen, signalmen) looking down on those who worked at the stations. But within the station staff, there was another hierarchy. The stationmaster was the supreme head and held middle-class status, wearing a frock coat and top hat. Beneath him were the booking clerks and a multitude of porters: goods porters, office porters, letter porters, lamp porters and so on. A large city station, such as Bristol or Bath, could have as many as 100 staff, in stark contrast to the small stations such as Wanstrow, near Frome, on the Great Western line. That little station had no staff at all and when its five trains a day stopped there, it was a platelayer who would light the lamps and the waiting-room fire in the evenings.

There was a family atmosphere, often with generations of the same family being employed by the same company. A father working for the Somerset & Dorset would expect his son to be offered a position when the time came. There was also a family atmosphere between employees and this was reflected in the way that so many stations were cared for as if they were homes, with neat and orderly flowerbeds – especially true of the S&D and West Somerset Railway stations – and kitchen gardens or allotments alongside the tracks maintained by the railway employees. It was therefore doubly tragic when in 1966 the Beeching cuts took their toll, with more than one member of the same family losing their income, and with the loss of the family atmosphere within the circle of working friendships.

6

BRIDGES, BRUNEL AND BERTHA

THE STEAM-DRIVEN TELESCOPIC BRIDGE

The penetration of the railway into Somerset brought with it great challenges for the engineers, Brunel in particular. With the Bristol & Exeter line travelling southwards across the county, it needed to cross the River Parrett just south of Bridgwater. As brilliant as the man was, he didn't always get it right first time. In constructing the Somerset Bridge across the river, he first had stone buttresses built on foundations set in the heavy clay soil, and then a stone arched bridge constructed on those buttresses. Under the stress of the arched bridge, the foundations shifted and he had to revise the design, replacing it with a timber bridge. A different challenge had to be faced further down the river where a branch line to the nearby docks crossed the river.

In 1840/41 the canal from Taunton reached Bridgwater at the newly constructed docks, on one side of the river, whilst the railway arrived on the other. Hence a branch line was needed to link the two. The problem was that the branch line had to cross the river downstream from the old Town Bridge. Between this bridge and the new railway bridge were two quaysides where trading ships moored up. These tall-masted ships would be unable to reach the quaysides once a railway bridge was thrown across the river. A solution was required that satisfied all parties concerned. A bridge was designed which we know today as the Black Bridge.

It was a steam-driven telescopic bridge supported on two large piers, one each side of the river. When ships came up the river, a section of the rail track on the east bank would be slid sideways into an otherwise open space alongside the track. This then created a gap where the line had previously been, which provided the space for a section of the bridge to be retracted back, rolling on small wheels that can still be seen beneath the bridge. The whole exercise was powered by a steam-driven engine housed at the riverside. The engine survives in the care of the Westonzoyland Engine Trust.

MUD, GLORIOUS MUD

Another problem, waiting for a steam-driven solution, was the mud in the docks. With a 30-foot tidal rise and fall, the River Parrett is heavily laden with silt. Ships entering from the river would pass through a lock gate into the outer basin, and then another into the inner basin of the docks. Each entry allowed the silt to rush in, where it would accumulate on the basin floor, reducing the effective depth of the dock. The original plan to overcome this problem was a system of 'flushes'. Around the dock basin, volumes of water were held in reserve and then simultaneously released into the dock. It was similar to a toilet being flushed with the water swirling around. The idea was to stir up the silt at low tide and then open the lock

Brunel-designed Bertha, *Bridgwater's mud dredger.*

gates to the river to let the silt-laden water run out. It failed and a Brunel solution was required.

His contribution was the design of *Bertha*, the steam-driven dredger. The concept was simple. Imagine if the dock was completely drained and a bulldozer was used to push the silt deposit to the river end of the dock. The bulldozer blade is down in one direction and up in the other. That was how *Bertha* worked but as a floating vessel. She had a large vertical beam, which could be raised and lowered. At the bottom end was a 'bulldozer' blade that shifted the mud down to the lock gates from where it could be flushed into the river. *Bertha* ran up and down a length of chain from one end of the dock to the other. At the end of each journey, the chain would be moved a bit further across the dock, so that over a period of several up-and-down trips, she covered the entire dock basin. It was a never-ending challenge but it solved the problem, thanks to Brunel's ingenuity.

The back end of the Eroder *with its water cannon nozzle can be seen just beyond the lock gate.*

The steam-driven paddle tug Petrel *at Carver's boatyard on the River Parrett.*

Sadly, when the docks closed, *Bertha* was neglected until rescued by the Exeter Maritime Museum. They twice went into liquidation and *Bertha* found a temporary home in the docks at Bristol before being acquired by the Maritime Museum in Lowestoft, where she has since been restored.

Tugs, water cannon and steam cranes

Elsewhere around the dock, steam provided other solutions. It was steam that drove some of the dockside cranes. The *Eroder* and the *Pioneer* were boats fitted with water cannon to blast mud from the quaysides. This simple but effective method kept the river banks and moorings clear of silt. Manufactured locally, at Bridgwater's W. & F. Wills engineering works, they gave loyal service from 1894 to 1927. Also operating along the river were the steam-powered paddled-driven tugs, such as the *Petrel*, which were used to replace the hobblers, men of a very hardy breed who would manually haul ships up the river, pulling them by ropes to their mooring places.

7

RADSTOCK TRAIN DISASTER

The **Bank Holiday started** full of promise but, by the end of the following day, sixteen-year-old Alfred Dando would be unfairly arrested for causing the death of twelve people from the Radstock area. At 11.20 pm on 7th August 1876, the Somerset & Dorset line was to suffer its worst-ever rail disaster. With hindsight, it was predictable, so slack was the training and so inadequate the execution of operating procedures. Even today, there still remains confusion as to exactly who did what and what went wrong. There were so many individuals involved in this farce that everyone was blaming everyone else and the truth was proving elusive.

Two years prior to the disaster, the Somerset & Dorset Railway opened an extension from Evercreech to Bath. It proved expensive, both in financial terms as well as human life. At Winsor Hill, two tunnels of over 240 yards had to be cut. During the excavation, a rockfall crushed four of the navvies engaged in the tunnelling operation. Their bodies were recovered and buried in Shepton Mallet's cemetery, where their grave is marked by a monument carved from the very rock that caused their deaths. The cost of this line had left the rail company almost bankrupt. A year later, the line was leased to the Midland and the London & South Western Railways, just a month before the accident. During this transition, no one company took full responsibility for ensuring the organised and safe running of the line, or if they had, then safe practices had not yet had chance to become part of the culture. The organisation was understaffed and over-stretched. On the day concerned, the rail traffic was exceptionally heavy. As it was a bank holiday, with numerous special excursions organised, 17 extra trains had been laid on, over and above what was already a busy schedule.

The line from Bath to Evercreech included a stretch of single track. Along the route, there were passing points, crossing loops, where one train takes a side line while another passes through on the main line. This not only caters for trains going in opposite directions, but also allows faster trains to overtake the slower ones. These loops were normally controlled with a manned signal at each end, with telegraphic communication between them. On this stretch of line, there were crossing loops at Radstock and Wellow stations, about four miles apart. In 1875, midway between the two mentioned stations, a branch line was introduced, allowing traffic into the Braysdown Colliery. This was given a signal box, at Foxcote, which effectively split the Radstock to Wellow section into two. Whilst it might be expected that all of these signal positions should be able to communicate with each other, that was not the case. Radstock could not communicate with Wellow, nor vice versa, but they could both communicate with Foxcote, which lay between them, and hence messages could be relayed from one to the other via Foxcote.

The men at the stations and the signal box were not responsible for the overall control of the movement of trains, only for the trains into and out of their own sections. Overall control was held by the 'crossing agent, Caleb Percy at Glastonbury, whose role it was to ensure the safe passage of trains across the network. Sadly, whilst the crossing agent could communicate by telegraph with Wellow and Radstock, he could not communicate with Foxcote. And herein we can see a picture building up of an inadequate, ill-prepared, creaking system. Add to this the fact that at the three critical points in this episode, the oldest person involved was only 18 years old. The youngest, Arthur Hillard, was only 15 and 16-year-old Alfred Dando at Foxcote, could hardly read or write and wasn't strong enough to properly move the signal levers!

With 17 extra trains on the schedule, Caleb Percy was having a stressful day. Pretty well everyone involved in this story had already been working for at least 12 hours. The disaster was about to unfold. An unscheduled up-train was on its way from Bournemouth to Bath. It had been laid on at short notice to follow a scheduled train that had proved to be overcrowded. A down-train full of passengers was returning to Radstock from a regatta at Bath. It was eleven hours behind schedule. Caleb Percy was unaware of the whereabouts of either of these trains. No arrangements had been made for either of them to cross on the single line between Wellow and Radstock.

He telegraphed an enquiry to Wellow, asking if they were aware of the down-train. Arthur Hillard, the 15-year-old telegraph boy, had been left in sole charge of the station, none of the senior staff being there at the time. His response was that the stationmaster had gone for a drink! The reply from Radstock was equally vague.

When the up-train reached Radstock, the stationmaster sent her through to Foxcote without any crossing orders being given. Approaching the Foxcote signals, the driver brought his train to a stop. The signals were confusing. The signal arm was halfway between safe and caution, because the signal boy lacked the strength to get the arm in either position correctly. The signal lamp was only just visible because Dando had not been given enough oil to keep it going. So there was Dando conscientiously standing at the side of the track waving a hand-held lamp. A few minutes later, and believing that the preceding up-train was now clear of the next section, he signalled the driver of the up-train to proceed. No one at Wellow had told him that a down-train was being sent down the single track from the other direction. As the down-train approached Foxcote, driver John Hamlin was making good speed on the downhill gradient but was unable to see the dimly lit signal ahead and, too late, was faced with the oncoming up-train, just 30 yards away.

The deafening crash, which was heard five miles away, was followed by piercing whistles of two engines letting off steam, head-to-head like rutting stags, horns locked, still on the rails with just one wheel off the track between them. These robustly-built engines were to survive and give many more years of service, but not so lucky were twelve of the passengers, including an eight-week-old baby. The first six of the fourteen carriages on the down-train were completely destroyed and it was within these that all the casualties were to be found, twelve dead and twenty-nine injured. Both drivers survived. Thirty-eight-year-old Anna Maria Chivers left eight children motherless. William Godfrey, George Saunders and William Goulding, who all worked at the Bell Inn in Radstock, perished along with their wives. The bodies were taken to the nearby Paglinch Farm where they were laid out in the granary prior to their identification and the first stage of the inquest.

In their attempts to switch the blame away from themselves, everyone involved appeared to be blaming Alfred Dando at the Foxcote signal box.

When there are so many things to go wrong, one of them will – and in this case, they all went wrong at the same time. Dando was arrested but later released and found to be blameless. He continued his career with the S&D where he was described as a quiet man who read his bible every day.

Jarrett, the stationmaster at Radstock, should never have sent the up-train forward without knowing the location of the down-train. He was severely censured, as was the Glastonbury-based Caleb Percy. Hillard, the telegraph boy at Wellow, should not have accepted the up-train having just sent the down-train into the system. James Sleep, the stationmaster at Wellow, was identified as being at greatest fault. The evidence given by Hillard and Sleep was in direct contradiction of each other. Poor Hillard, at just fifteen years old, had worked for over 15 hours that day and had been left unsupervised for at least five hours and with far too many jobs to see to, handling telegraphs, issuing tickets and keeping accounts. Yet here he was receiving the blame. The following March, Sleep was charged with manslaughter and, having been found guilty, sentenced to twelve months in prison.

The Somerset & Dorset's name had been tarnished forever. 'Slow and Dirty' and other S&D phrases became the standard taunt, justifiably given but unfair in the longer term when the S&D improved its service beyond recognition. Their first steps towards atonement for the disaster was to give each orphaned child a bible, and where there was more than one child in the family, an extra five shillings per child. Later, all those orphans were employed by the company. One widow received £1,000 in compensation.

Sixty years later, in July 1936, a further incident was to take place at the same spot. Fortunately this one was without the tragedy of the earlier episode and, in its own way, was a comedy of errors worthy of a *Thomas the Tank Engine* tale!

INSPIRATION FOR THOMAS

PERCY RUNS AWAY

Only a classic film in the style of an Ealing comedy could provide justice to this story of a great railway farce, which fortunately fell short of a full-scale disaster. Indeed, such was the comedy element, that the Rev W.V. Awdry incorporated his version in the *Thomas the Tank Engine* series of books. 'Percy Runs Away' relates how Percy, Thomas's smaller friend, forgot to warn the signalman before Gordon arrived with the express train, a mistake that resulted in Percy being knocked backwards and running away driverless. As incredible as the Rev Awdry's story may appear, the actual incident on which it was based was even more unbelievable.

It was 29th July 1936 when locomotive 7620, a tank engine at the head of eight wagons, was being shunted by its driver named Ash at the Braysdown Colliery in the north of the county. Meanwhile a freight train, whose driver was named Brewer, had just passed signals at danger close to the Writhlington signal box near Radstock. The error on the part of the freight driver put the two engines on the same track and heading towards each other. The reactions from the two drivers, on realising the impending disaster, were not only unexpected but in complete contrast to each other.

Aware of the possible consequences, and fearful for their lives, both the freight train driver Brewer and his fireman Hiroms leapt from the footplate to relative safety, leaving their engine heading towards the oncoming tank engine. Unfortunately they had not fully closed down the regulator, which is the train driver's equivalent to leaving the foot slightly on the accelerator. A panicky attempt to put the engine into reverse had also failed and it slipped back into forward gear. Ash, the driver of the tank engine, threw his engine into reverse and, as soon as it made contact with the trailing wagons, opened the regulator to full. As the wheels screamed on the rails, the engine lost its forward movement and was at the turning point where it was about to go into reverse. The driver of the tank engine realised that the freight train was moving relatively slowly towards him. He had already witnessed the rapid disappearance of the driver and fireman from the other engine and was undoubtedly amazed at their dereliction of duty. He, fortunately, was made of sterner stuff and showed great initiative in the action that followed.

He had realised that the other engine was going slowly enough that, if he could get alongside her, he could leap on board and bring her to a halt, like the hero in a Western movie leaping onto the horses of a runaway stagecoach. Oh the glory, the fame that this daring adventure would bring him! He would be famous throughout the railway world, a hero whose name would be emblazoned across the front pages of the national newspapers.

With his own engine now going into reverse, its pace was slow enough to allow him to jump off and run up the track to reach the freight engine where he would save the day. Jumping from the footplate, he sprinted as fast as his legs would carry him and leapt aboard the freight engine and, taking the controls, brought it safely to a halt. He must have been aglow with satisfaction. Surely such outstanding initiative and courage were worthy of some high honour.

Unfortunately he had forgotten to explain his plan to Parker, his fireman, who, having seen him leap from the train so soon after the driver and the fireman of the freight engine had done the same, assumed that his driver had likewise abandoned ship, presumably fearing for his own life. Not one to go down alone with the sinking ship, he likewise leapt from the footplate as his engine slowly increased its pace, now heading backwards towards Bath.

The tank engine driver, now in control of the freight engine, could only watch in horror as he saw his fireman standing alongside the track watching their tank engine disappear into the distance, pushing the eight wagons before her. Considering she had neither driver nor fireman, she made quite good progress, with a clear line most of the way to Bath. Merrily she sped through Wellow station. The time to reach Midford, some five miles away, was very impressive but beyond there the situation declined rapidly. With the benefit of a downhill gradient, her speed increased and was estimated at 50 miles per hour as she shot past Midford station, her wagons rattling and bouncing on the lines. But ahead the points were against her and 7620 managed to derail most of what she was pushing. Bravely she pressed on, determined to show her capabilities. Six of her wagons went careering down a bank, finishing up in the garden of a pub, a dishevelled pile of tangled wreckage. Meanwhile 7620, proudly speeding along and shunting two derailed wagons before her, demolished telegraph poles like tumbling skittles, with signals being shown no more respect as they likewise toppled in her path. A nearby house just escaped demolition as another thrown-away wagon came to a halt just a few yards from its door. Not even the signal box could do anything to slow her progress and was partly demolished for daringly trying.

Relentlessly 7620 pressed on towards Bath, determined to reach her destination, with one last loyal wagon staying with her until the bitter end. It was a painful journey as, bolt by bolt, the wagon fell apart like a car in a demolition derby. Even losing one of her axles didn't stop her. She just continued on two wheels. Onwards they sped, negotiating first the single track Combe Down tunnel, unaffected by the darkness within, and then the Devonshire tunnel until, now back into the light of day, the finishing line was in sight. They had travelled over five miles together and reached a point where the line merged with another. Then, like a steeplechaser who falls at the final hurdle, as she reached the connecting points, 7620 stumbled over her one remaining wagon and fell off the rails almost within sight of the old ticket platform for Bath Junction. The wagon's one remaining door fell off and went under her wheels. It was at the entrance to the Claude Avenue over-bridge. Amazingly the only damage to the tank engine was superficial; the bunker plating was bent and a few pipes were broken.

There was no glorious reception for the tank engine driver – but the tank engine was immortalised in the Rev Awdry's 'Percy Runs Away'.

NEIL, THE BOX TANK ENGINE

When iron ore mining commenced on the Brendon Hills, a railway line was required to carry the extracted ore from the hills to the harbour town of Watchet, from where it would be taken to Newport and on to Ebbw Vale for smelting. The first engine to serve the line was a Nielson 'box' engine, aptly named as old images reveal. It was a saddle tank with very rectangular outlines. This arrival was shortly followed by another engine of the same design but the almost perfect rectangular forms were slightly altered within a matter of months when the two engines collided in what was to be a fatal accident in August 1857. One engine had to be scrapped and the other remained derelict for some while to come, having been lucky enough to have already survived a previous disaster when an inexperienced crew member fired up the engine having forgotten to put any water in the boiler!

However, the reason for including the 'box' here is that she was the inspiration for Thomas the Tank Engine's friend and colleague Neil. Neil appears in 'Very Old Engines', where he was dark green with 'S&M 2'

West Somerset Mineral Railway's 'box' tank.
(Courtesy of West Somerset Steam Railway Trust)

painted on the side of his panniers and was described as ugly and simple, but of a very kind nature.

Gordon opens up a panoramic window

Other episodes around the county were to inspire stories for the *Thomas the Tank Engine* series. In Bridgwater, in the sidings on what is now the Colley Lane industrial estate, a Metro tank engine, number 5812, was raising steam. Maybe because it was still very early in the morning and those in attendance were not fully awake, but whatever the cause, the regulator had been left opened and the effect of this was that, as the pressure of steam increased, the engine slowly, and unattended, began to move. Approaching the rear wall of the shed, it jumped its stop-blocks and came to a halt with its smoke box and funnel projecting through the rear wall with the front driving wheels suspended in the air about twenty feet above the pavement below, as though it were a raging rhino attempting to escape captivity. Fortunately the damage was limited to a pile of bricks in the road and a large amount of egg on the faces of those involved. But at least the engine shed now had a panoramic window in one end and provided inspiration for 'A Better View for Gordon'. In the Rev Awdry version of this tale, it was Gordon who opened up the view. Gordon was a powerful engine with the important responsibility of pulling passenger trains. He was pompous and arrogant. He looked down on tank engines, which were only fit for shunting. 'Tender engines don't shunt' was his philosophy. He was the kind of character associated with 'pride comes before a fall'. In the episode concerned, Gordon is in a brand new engine shed, testing out the line. He is getting bored, staring at the plaster on the wall in front of his buffers, and is 'taken ill'. Repaired, he returns to the shed in time for the opening, but loses control and crashes straight through the wall. Eventually he returns to the shed, which, by then, had been repaired and now featured a panoramic window. No longer would he be bored staring at the plaster.

Percy Takes the Plunge

'Percy's Promise' in series 11 tells how Thomas's train is marooned by floods, but manages to get to the station. Compare this with the flooded line at

Floods are a regular occurrence near Creech St Michael.

Creech St Michael in November 1894 and the fictitious story mirrors the reality. In series 12 'Percy Takes the Plunge' tells how Percy gets the trucks to push him past a 'danger' board and ends up in the sea, reflecting the story from Burnham-on-Sea where a contractor's locomotive ran off the end of the jetty.

9

THE RUNAWAYS

THE FUMES OF THE COMBE DOWN TUNNEL

The Combe Down tunnel, built in 1874, is on the old Somerset & Dorset line between Midford and Bath's Green Park. Travelling towards Bath, the approach to the tunnel has an upward gradient of 1 in 100 and on the other side a decline running down to Bath. A mile in length, it is the longest unventilated tunnel in the country, and therein lay part of its problem. The cost of carving the tunnel out of the hillside was sufficient to bankrupt the company responsible and so it remained single track. Being long, narrow and totally lacking in ventilation, fumes were a problem for slow trains labouring up the enclosed incline. It was an accident waiting to happen.

On 20th November 1929 the almost new engine, number 89, was at the head of a freight train, running with its tender first from Evercreech up to the goods yard at Bath. The journey would take them though the Combe Down tunnel where the unfortunate events of that day were about to unfold. Trains had been passing through that same tunnel for fifty years with no problems, so why should it all go wrong on that fateful day? It was an unfortunate once-in-a-lifetime combination of circumstances.

As they left Evercreech, engine 89 was creating more smoke than usual and Driver Harry Jennings commented on this to his fireman, Maurice Pearce. They journeyed on to Radstock where they dropped some empty wagons and picked up loaded ones, adding to their already heavy load. Once again they discussed the engine's poor performance. Going over the Masbury incline, they took 13 minutes longer than expected and concern grew as they approached the Combe Down tunnel. Before that, they had to pass through Wellow and Midford. Christopher Wagner, the guard, suggested that perhaps when they reached Wellow, they should ask that they be granted a clear run through Midford so that they could have sufficient momentum as they approached the tunnel, momentum which would be lost if they had to stop at Midford. Jennings sent a message, via the porter at Radstock, to the signalman at Wellow but it couldn't be arranged because a passenger train was already on the line.

While they were waiting at Midford, Pearce did everything he could to get the best power, clearing the clinkers and tending the fire. As they left Midford, their speed built up to 15 mph but such was the gradient approaching the Combe Down tunnel that they entered it at just 4 mph. This was a fraction of the usual speed, which meant they would be in the tunnel for some 12 to 15 minutes instead of the usual four or five. It was a humid day, with little air moving. Normally the speed of the train would take all the engine fumes away from the crew on board, but at 4 mph they clung around the cab. In the narrow tunnel, the engine funnels were within an inch or two of the roof. There was nowhere for the fumes to go.

Crowds watch Great Western engine 212 testing Arthur Reginald Angus's automatic signal control system on the Minehead line at Kentsford in 1912.
(Courtesy of West Somerset Steam Railway Trust)

And here we must make some suppositions as to what occurred. We know that the fireman and the guard both complained that the heat was exceptional. The noise from the struggling engine was deafening. Shortly after entering the tunnel, Maurice Pearce, the fireman, who was from Midsomer Norton, had to wrap his coat around his head and curl up on the floor to protect himself from the heat and fumes. Coughing violently, he collapsed in an unconscious heap on the footplate. In all probability, it was as the engine struggled through the tunnel that the fumes also overcame the driver. The carbon monoxide levels in his blood had built to a level sufficient to knock out the strongest individual. With both driver and fireman collapsed on the footplate, the engine slowed to a crawling pace. At the rear of the train, Wagner, the guard, aware of the stifling heat and fumes, held his lantern to the tunnel wall just to make sure they were still moving. By the time the engine emerged into the mid-afternoon daylight, both driver and fireman were totally unconscious. Finally the engine took advantage of its full head of steam and the steep two-mile decline towards Bath.

Wagner at the rear, on seeing the daylight, listened for the sound of the wagon couplings, indicating that the fully stretched load was closing up as it tipped from uphill to down. No sound came. The engine had begun to accelerate to the extent that the wagons never caught up with each other but remained at full stretch as the train started to speed towards the Bath goods yard, gathering pace as she ran down the bank from the tunnel. Wagner, realising that the train was out of control, knew that there was nothing he could do. He leapt from the train, looking after his own safety but receiving serious injuries in the process, both his legs being broken.

With 37 loaded wagons, in total weighing nearly 500 tons, plus the brake van, derailment was inevitable. Down in the goods yard, railway workers could only watch as the train sped recklessly towards them. Young Jack Loader, a clerk from Gloucester, was taking a short cut across the yard. Nearby was the yard's Inspector, John Norman. He shouted a warning for everyone to get well away and he ran back towards the Clearing House. As the train derailed, debris flew like shrapnel, killing Jack Loader. The engine careered on until, at 60 mph, it collided with and completely wrecked the rear end of a building used by the Clearing House staff, where Inspector Norman had just arrived. He also became a fatal victim of the flying debris. The engine lay on its side. The 37 wagons concertinaed up into a giant pile of wreckage, only the brake van remaining upright. In the demolished shed, a gas pipe ruptured and the threat of an explosion hung over the rescue party. A stove inside the shed had been knocked sideways as the building crumbled, scattering burning coals across the grounds, setting fire to the timbers of the building and in turn igniting the escaping gas. Other burning coals shot through the air towards a terrace of housing that lined the railway embankment. As they crashed through upstairs windows, a number of small fires were ignited, one of which was on the bed of three-year-old Joan Carpenter, who was snatched to safety by her mother.

Rail staff rushed towards the scene of the devastation. The tender, which was at the head of the train, was lying on its side in a deep depression carved out by its bumpers. Steam was blasting out of the engine and a jet of gas flame was threatening the rescue party. William Bowles, the driver of a passenger train that had just arrived from Templecombe, crawled through the coal hole of the tender, the only way the engine cab could be accessed. Initially he could see nothing except for one of Pearce's legs. He felt for and found a pulse but Pearce's clothes were already alight as he lay with his coat wrapped around his head and under a pile of burning coals. Despite the risk of an explosion, Bowles persevered and beneath the body of Pearce found the body of Driver Jennings. His clothes too were ablaze. Beating out the flames on one and brushing away the burning coals from the other, Bowles managed to drag them out, both still alive but only just. Jennings died a few minutes later on his way to hospital. The unconscious Pearce was likewise deemed to be dead and his wife in Midsomer Norton was notified. Her grief turned to relief when she arrived at the hospital to find that reports of her husband's death had been exaggerated. He was, however, badly burned but was able to be released from the Royal United Hospital at Bath several weeks later.

It was a combination of unfortunate circumstances: a heavy load, having to stop, a poorly performing engine, the timing of the passenger train, humid atmosphere, no ventilation chimneys in the tunnel. They all coincided to create the conditions leading to the accident. A recommendation that ventilation in the tunnel should be improved was ignored – too expensive. The only accepted recommendation was that such large loads should in future be reduced. It was the cheapest option!

HALF GOES ONE WAY, HALF THE OTHER

Despite that recommendation, the practice of overloading engines was to continue. In 1948 Leo Elkins, as driver, and Ron Hatcher, as fireman, were taking an ammunition train to Bath and had made good time from Evercreech to Binegar. At Midford, they picked up the token that allowed them onto the single track as they approached the Combe Down tunnel. For some unknown reason, their engine was lacking power and had almost come to a halt as they approached the tunnel entrance. Ron Hatcher looked back towards the guard's van and to his horror could see its guard lamp gradually moving away from them, gaining in speed in the wrong direction. Somewhere a coupling had come adrift partway along the train and the back half and front half were heading in opposite directions. The driver put the engine into reverse; a quick phone call was made from the first available trackside phone to the signalman at Midford. He was alerted to the approaching carriages and gave permission for the driver to reverse back to pick up the runaways.

They eventually re-connected with the errant wagons but now, having lost all momentum, knew that their load would be too heavy to complete the uphill part of the journey. A few hours later an extra engine arrived to escort them. It was a late arrival home for the driver but the fireman's day was yet to get worse. Whether it was a flying cinder or a carelessly disposed of cigarette butt, we will never know, but by the time Ron Hatcher had freshened up and made ready for bed, he could smell smoke. His raincoat, by now hung up in a cupboard, was smouldering nicely. Ron grabbed it and threw it out through the door into the rain. The rush of air as it left the house was sufficient to fan the flames and that was the end of Ron's raincoat. A perfect end to a perfect day? Certainly one he would prefer to forget.

THE NORTON FITZWARREN JINX

THE 1890 BOAT TRAIN DISASTER

Three fatal accidents took place on one stretch of the Great Western line. Whilst none would qualify individually as top-ten ranking disasters, the combined effect must put this bit of line amongst the highest for rail accident fatalities, 51 in total plus over a hundred others injured, and yet they are spread over a period of almost ninety years. There is no common link to say that their presence on the same stretch of line is anything other than pure coincidence.

The first accident occurred in the early hours of the morning on 11th November 1890. The previous evening, the *Norham Castle* had sailed into Plymouth harbour with her fifty or so passengers from Cape Town, South Africa. Their 19-day voyage had been particularly difficult, experiencing violent weather, the kind that binds individuals together in the face of adversity. They had become a close group of friends despite their various backgrounds and nationalities. They were relieved to leave the ship and board the overnight train from Plymouth to Paddington, unaware that their journey was to be even more eventful and even more terrifying. They were well-to-do, mostly travelling first-class at the head of the train, with one second class carriage and the brake van the only other carriages. They were making good time as they approached Norton Fitzwarren, just a couple of miles from Taunton, at about half past one in the morning, but that was about to change.

A slow goods train with 39 wagons and a brake van had arrived at Norton Fitzwarren, heading down the line from Bristol to Exeter, but stopping at Norton to drop some wagons and pick up others. With a faster down-train expected just minutes behind her, the slow goods train was ordered to cross over onto the up line to let the fast down-train through. The fast train having passed, the down line was now clear for the slow goods train to return to the down and leave the up line free for the approaching passenger train.

It was then that George Rice, the operator of the nearby signal box, received the message that the special boat train from Plymouth was arriving. It seems he simply forgot that the slow goods train was still on the up line and cleared the signal allowing the special passenger train to pass straight through, sending her headlong into the waiting goods train. In his defence, he claimed that he had a bad head that night. Some three months before, he had been knocked over by an engine, leaving him with broken ribs and a head injury. He had been suffering from headaches ever since and was on medication. The situation was additionally complicated by the fact that the driver of the goods train had changed his lamp from red to green, to indicate that he was back on his proper line, ie not the up line. The driver and fireman, seeing a green light, would have anticipated a clear run but then, realising what was about to happen, they leapt from the engine to relative safety. In similar fashion, Charles Noble and Alfred Dowling, driver and fireman of the goods train, leapt to safety when the passenger train was just 100 yards away and closing in fast.

In the first carriage of the passenger train, Max Heimann of Hanover had spent much of the journey in conversation with a fellow passenger, Mr Wells of Shepherd's Bush, London, but Mr Wells by now had fallen asleep. In another compartment, Mr T.W. Bussey sat facing the engine when there was then the horrifying sound of the crash and a blaze of light. He was launched from his seat to hit the carriage on the opposite side. The tender of the goods train was smashed to smithereens, three of its wagons were destroyed and nine more badly damaged. The front carriage of the passenger train was completely wrecked, the engine of the train having broken through six of its seven compartments. The second carriage and the brake van were also badly damaged. Ten passengers lay dead and a further eleven were badly injured, including the driver and fireman.

To make matters worse, the passenger carriage caught fire and began to fill with smoke. Mr Wells, badly cut about the head and with severe chest injuries, lay unconscious, unaware of what had happened until he regained consciousness the following morning, when he discovered that

Max Heimann had not been so lucky. Heimann had been killed instantly and a fellow German named Cohen had also died, having literally lost his head in the crash. Also decapitated was the son of a black Wesleyan missionary from the Eastern Cape whose remains were buried in St Mary's at Taunton. The following day, Taunton was abuzz with rumours of the disaster and the interest generated was sufficient to justify an excursion train to visit the site.

The 1940 disaster

Fifty years later, almost to the day, disaster struck once more. It was 4th November 1940. It was wartime and the London-based driver, P.W. Stacey, was undoubtedly suffering from sleepless nights during the air raids. Just hours before leaving for the fateful journey, his own house had been hit. As a result of that night's raid, he was more than an hour late leaving Paddington in control of engine number 6028, *King George VI*. His now delayed passenger train had pulled in 68 minutes late at Taunton station, where there were two lines in each direction, to give four parallel tracks. There were two inner tracks, one for the up and one for the down line. These were for the faster trains, with the outer tracks for the slower, stopping traffic. A fast newspaper train was coming in behind him and he was moved to the left from the inner to outer track to let the faster train through. Some two miles down the line, at Norton Fitzwarren, the two tracks merged as one.

Before pulling out of Taunton station, in the darkness of the blackout, he checked the signals to see if he could safely proceed, but forgot that he was on the relief line. In the darkness of the blackout conditions, he mistook the 'all clear' green light of the fast track for his own signal and pulled out of Taunton station. He had 900 passengers on board, many of them servicemen. As he approached the points where the two tracks merged as one at Norton Fitzwarren, and now doing about 45 miles per hour, he was overtaken by the faster newspaper train and realised too late that he was on the down relief line, not the main, and that the points would be against him. He applied the brakes but it was beyond hope. The engine hit the catch points and was instantly thrown clear and landed on its left-hand side, almost 50 yards away, killing his fireman. The first five carriages, two of which had overtaken the engine, were wrecked and laid strewn in a chaotic pile across the rails, blocking all the tracks. The third carriage was jammed against the tender and the fifth had compacted for half of its length into the third and sixth carriages. It was a scene of total devastation.

Incredibly the guard of the newspaper train was almost unaware of the chaos behind but did hear an unexplained sound. He signalled his driver to stop his train to check for damage under the 'Stop and Examine' rule, which should always be applied when any strange sound or vibration is felt. By this time, in the darkness, they were well out of sight of the wrecked train and proceeded totally unaware of the disaster behind them where 27 had been killed, including 13 sailors, and 75 others injured in the crash that was one of the country's worst-ever rail disasters. Amongst the fatalities were the variety artist Archie Lewis and his wife, Archie being a popular wartime entertainer.

Within 45 minutes the emergency services had arrived, having been called by the stationmaster at Norton Fitzwarren, but meanwhile the uninjured passengers were doing their bit. Fortunately a Surgeon Commander was amongst the military personnel on board. He and his wife had just been bombed out of their Bromley home and were on their way to stay with their daughter who had been evacuated to Helston. He was able to help some of the injured. Local residents turned up in force, with various tools, some of which they had collected from the nearby ganger's hut. Perhaps it was because they were growing used to wartime conditions that there appeared to be complete composure in what one could expect to be chaotic conditions in a scene of total carnage. The 27 dead and 75 injured were taken to hospital in Taunton.

TAUNTON SLEEPING CAR DISASTER, 1978

It was another disaster waiting to happen. Sleeping carriage number W2437 was a British Railways Mark 1 coach built in 1960. Its heating was provided by the steam from the engine. It was safe and well proven. By the 1970s, early attempts at maintaining steam heating by having boilers in the diesel engines had proved expensive and unsuccessful. Consequently, in 1976, carriage number W2437 had been converted to electric heating with the heater installed in the vestibule.

On 5th July 1978 the overnight sleeper to Paddington arrived at Plymouth from Penzance. Bed linen was formerly kept in plastic bags in the guard's van at the rear of the train, but in more recent years the guard's vans had been dropped. Consequently the plastic bags containing the used linen were stored in the vestibule of W2437, next to the electric heater. It was only a matter of time before disaster would strike.

At just after midnight, and a quarter of an hour before the train pulled out from Plymouth, the heating was switched on. No one had noticed any problems as they took their scheduled stops at Newton Abbot and Exeter, but the bags were already heating up to a critical temperature. Journeying towards Taunton, they were giving off toxic fumes including carbon monoxide. These were fed through the air conditioning to the sleeping compartments. At about twenty to three in the morning, fire broke out and the communication cord was pulled. They were just passing Norton Fitzwarren and the train came to a halt about a mile further on, a mile short of Taunton station, near the Silk Mills signal box. The driver jumped down from the footplate to look back and saw the fire. Conveniently he had stopped almost adjacent to a trackside telephone, which he used to call the signal box. 'Stop everything. Get the fire brigade and ambulance. The sleeper is on fire,' he ordered.

By now most of the twelve victims were already dead from carbon monoxide poisoning. The first sleeper carriage was completely gutted by the fire, and both smoke and flames had already spread to the second. Some passengers woke and, realising what was happening, made their escape with some difficulty as they struggled through the heat and smoke. The sleeping car attendant who had pulled the cord warned as many passengers as he could before he too was overcome by smoke.

When the local fire brigade arrived, four minutes after being summoned, they discovered that both the internal and external doors of the carriages had been locked, to avoid any intruders during the overnight journey. It was an illegal but nonetheless common practice. Whilst it was usual to lock the doors between the carriages overnight, the external doors should have been left unlocked. The local police had already arrived ahead of the fire brigade and had begun the evacuation of the coaches beyond the inaccessible front two. Police Constable Ryan, hearing voices from the second carriage, managed to get in through a broken window. Inside he crawled through the choking smoke but could find only empty compartments. Driven back by the heat, he escaped to find two firemen with breathing apparatus. They entered the carriage and returned with the unconscious body of a man who was then resuscitated and taken away by ambulance.

Mr B.J. Nightingale was one lucky escapee. He had been the sole occupant of berths 1 and 2, right next to the source of the fire. He woke up as the train came to a standstill to find his compartment so hot that it took his breath away. As he tried to smash his way out through the window, someone from outside shouted for him to stay low, to get below the gases and to crawl to safety. Grasping the handle of his compartment door, he burnt his hands but had to keep going since the ceiling of his berth was now ablaze and dripping burning material. In total darkness, he crawled towards the rear of the carriage, conscious of someone else crawling before him. He passed an unseen body on his way, eventually reaching the end of the carriage where he passed out. His next recollection was walking along the outside of the carriage.

Next to Mr Nightingale's berth was Mr C.J. Morley. He too had woken up, thanks to the smell of burning. Realising that the carriage was on fire, he left his compartment to see the berth to his left, Nightingale's, well ablaze. He ducked down beneath the fumes and headed away from the fire. In the darkness, he reached what he thought was the door to the next carriage but which with hindsight was probably the toilet. He lost consciousness and was another whose next memories were at the trackside. No one survived from berths 5 to 12. In berth 13, Surgeon Lieutenant-Commander G.H.G. McMillan of the Royal Navy awoke to the acrid smell of smoke and the sound of the ceiling of his berth ablaze. He knew from his naval training to keep low as he opened the door from his berth. The smoke-filled air hit his lungs, making it difficult to take a second breath. He crawled into the corridor and shouted: 'Get out, the train is on fire, get down on the floor.' It must have been his voice that Nightingale had heard. It was then that the lights went out. He crawled towards the rear of the carriage and felt a hand on his arm, presumably Nightingale. He told the other man to catch hold of his ankles and follow him out. Finding a door, he reached up to open the door or its windows but, unable to draw breath, fell back to the floor. He felt a naked foot against his face, presumably Mrs Drummond from berth 16. He was another whose next memory was when he regained consciousness at the trackside.

Eleven died in the disaster and a twelfth, a Belgian, was to die of pneumonia nine months later, never having regained consciousness. They were all in the first fourteen berths, those nearest the source of the fire. Nineteen others were injured, all from the front two carriages. For them it was a lucky escape with the carbon monoxide and gaseous cyanide gradually making its way along the carriage. Local residents from the nearby Fairwater Close rallied around with tea and blankets, taking survivors into their homes. The dead and wounded were transferred to Musgrove Park Hospital.

The survivors had their stories to tell, all of which came out at the subsequent enquiry. Mrs Drummond was one of those too traumatised by the experience to bear the pain of reciting their recollections of that night. As a result of their findings, a raft of changes were made to the future design of sleeper carriages and the rules regarding locked doors and training of staff were tightened.

NEVER WORK WITH ANIMALS OR MINERS

Most market towns across Somerset that had links with the railway had the facilities for handling cattle at the trackside. In my childhood, I well remember Bridgwater's cattle market, alongside which ran the main line from Bristol to Exeter, with its siding into the market. There, on a Wednesday morning, the cattle would be auctioned and those destined to travel further afield, perhaps to the Midlands, would be herded up the cattle ramp and into the cattle pens, pending collection.

Once in a while, one or more would escape. It was usually the farming community or slaughterhouse staff who would be rushing along the road to recover the errant beast, but sometimes it would be the uniformed railway staff giving chase. Cattle were frequently a problem on the lines, having strayed through a broken fence. On one occasion, the police shot an escaped bull on the railway line near Bridgwater, which caused a diplomatic incident since they had no authority on British Railways property.

During the years of the First World War, it was common to see horses being transferred by train, on their way to the battlefields of Europe. But these were not the only animals to travel by rail. Once in a while, more exotic species would be on the move.

BERTRAM MILLS' CIRCUS

What's the best way to move an elephant? When Bertram Mills' circus came to perform, it was by rail. In the 1950s, this circus was a regular visitor to the railway towns of Somerset. Their preparation and promotion was the same wherever they went. Taunton, Bridgwater and Yeovil all received the same treatment. The specially commissioned train would arrive and be taken into an appropriate siding. The circus paraphernalia was taken to the showground site, but the elephants would be bedecked with gold and red

Bertram Mills' Circus – the elephant procession in the 1950s.

robes whilst still in the sidings. Railway staff would gather around to watch the spectacle and laugh with delight as the elephants used their trunks to probe the pockets of the railwaymen, looking for treats.

Once they were ready, and the stilt-walkers were geared up, then off they'd go, heading into the town centre where they would parade through the streets, drawing the attention of both the crowds and the press. Inevitably most of their performances were sell-outs in those days when few of us had a television, and certainly no one that I knew.

THE ACCIDENT-PRONE WEST SOMERSET MINERAL RAILWAY

During the mid-19th century, iron ore was extracted from a mine at Gupworthy on the Brendon Hills. The ore was destined for smelting in South Wales but needed to get to Watchet Harbour first. Initially it was transported by horse-drawn wagons but in 1855 an act was passed allowing the construction of the West Somerset Mineral Railway. It was a completely independent railway, linking up with no other lines, and included a 1 in 4 gradient, an impossible gradient for any locomotive to manage. The solution depended on a regular supply of loaded wagons at the head of the incline. A rope connected the unloaded train going up with the loaded train going down, the rope passing over a pulley at the head of the incline. When mining stopped in 1883, and hence there were no loaded wagons going downhill, a steam engine had to be installed to do the hauling.

When the line opened in 1856, the railway company's first action was to cause the death of one of its own horses. The locomotive for the line had to be brought in by road, on a horse-drawn cart. The weight of the load was such that, on a downhill slope, the cart overtook and killed the horse that was hauling it. The engine's disastrous history didn't finish there. An inexperienced fireman lit the fire under the boiler without first having put any water in it. The engine was seriously damaged and a second engine had to be brought in whilst the first was being repaired. Within three months, disaster struck again.

In August 1857 the first engine was hauling a truckload of miners from Roadwater to get their pay. Meanwhile the second engine was coming towards them from the other end of the line; hence they were instructed to wait until they were cleared to continue. On the footplate of the waiting engine, the company's assistant engineer was too impatient and instructed the driver to go on. The two trains collided, killing three men whilst the escaping high-pressure steam caused severe burns to many others. Both engines were written off and a third engine had to be purchased.

Three years later, the railway company ran its first passenger service, but as there were no passenger carriages the 800 travellers, on their way to a temperance meeting, had to be carried in the goods wagons. For safety reasons, passengers were not allowed to travel up or down the 1 in 4 incline. The rail fare deliberately excluded that section. Nonetheless they were allowed to travel free of charge but at their own risk. But it was not only members of the Temperance Societies who travelled to Watchet on the train service; there was also many a thirsty miner. On the weekends, whole truckloads of them would descend from the hills onto the waiting harbour town. Meanwhile, ships from South Wales, bringing loads of culm, a low-grade and very dusty form of coal, would arrive leaving those who offloaded the vessels with lungs full of dust, which needed to be washed down. This mix of drunken miners and drunken sailors led to frequent

The steep incline at the West Somerset Mineral Railway, c.1907.
(Courtesy of West Somerset Steam Railway Trust)

evenings of pub brawls, more closely resembling the Wild West than the normal tranquillity of West Somerset. There is a local tale of one sailor whose wife regularly complained that her husband spent far too long in the pub 'clearing the dust' and once questioned him, in front of all his friends, as to why couldn't he just go into the pub and have twelve or fourteen pints like the other sailors and then go home. Why did he have to stay until he'd had a stomach full!

During the First World War, the decision was made to dismantle the now disused railway line to provide metal for the war effort. Much of this work was carried out by local sailors home on leave. The line was tackled from the far end first, bringing the removed rails back to Watchet. Trolleys were used that travelled along the track, propelled by muscle power. However, being sailors, it didn't take them long before they rigged up a boat's mast and a lugsail, and sailed off to work, enlisting help from the breeze.

THE WORLD LAND-SPEED RECORD

Few people would associate Somerset with the world land-speed record. Thoughts turn to racing cars on the salt flats of Utah, not to steam locomotives, let alone one pulling a full load of carriages in 1904!

It was 4th May and a day when one of those giant leaps for mankind was about to be leapt but then swept under the carpet. It was around twenty past eight in the morning. The Swindon-built *City of Truro* had picked up a trainload of transatlantic mail and passengers from San Francisco. They had just arrived at Plymouth docks. Five eight-wheeled postal vans were fully loaded at an estimated 148 tons, plus another 90 tons for the engine and tender. If she was being prepared for a record-breaking run, this was not the way to do it. But the City class engines were built for speed, like an athlete, not for power like her less elegant muscle-bound successors. For some while, there had been anticipation that a City class train would break the world speed record, and possibly even break the magic 100 mph barrier.

Pulling out of Plymouth, she began her run to London, with Bristol, at 128 miles away, being her first scheduled stop. That first leg of the journey was about to be completed in just over two hours and on board was Charles Rous-Marten, the timekeeper. After crossing the border into Somerset, the *City of Truro* passed through the Whiteball tunnel on her way to Wellington, on a run that would take her down the Wellington bank, a decline that gave her the opportunity for the record-breaking run. Rous-Marten, stopwatch in hand, looked out of the window. The tension in the cab must have been enormous as he meticulously took and recorded his timings. Along that short section of decline, they topped 102.3 mph, not only breaking the 100 mph barrier but smashing the world land-speed record.

The City of Truro *– world speed record breaker.*
(Courtesy of Gloucestershire Warwickshire Steam Railway plc)

What happened next? Did the world's press carry the banner headlines 'World Land-Speed Record Smashed'? No – this record to beat all records was hushed up. The Great Western Railway Company, which perhaps should have been singing its success from the rooftops, wanted to play the whole thing down. It was concerned about public reaction to what might be viewed as reckless behaviour. A recent rail disaster in Lancashire had heightened public worry about rail safety. The GWR was also competing with its rivals, the London & South Western, for the ocean mail traffic and considered that such recklessness might prejudice its chances for that long-term business.

A month later, Rous-Marten published an article in *The Railway Magazine*, giving details of the run but without the actual timings and with the comment: 'It is not desirable at present to publish the actual maximum rate that was reached on this memorable occasion.' Almost four years later, the table of timings and the maximum speed was finally published but not naming the engine concerned. It was not until April 1908 that all the details came together, in the magazine edition that coincided with Rous-Marten's death from a heart attack. But still the GWR failed to lay claim to the record.

Amazingly, it was another 30 years before the *Flying Scotsman* was to record a speed in excess of 100 mph. Some argue that it is the *Flying Scotsman* to whom the honours should be given, but if the National Railway

Museum at York give the prize to the *City of Truro*, that's good enough for me. For those who would like to view the *City of Truro*, she resides in the National Railway Museum, the only City class engine to avoid the scrapyard. There she has been well cared for, with a £130,000 refit being carried out in 2004. She also survives in the *Thomas the Tank Engine* stories where she is one of the rare band of real engines to run alongside the fictitious characters.

13

A HARD DAY'S NIGHT

In **December 2006** the old Great Western locomotive number 3850 was laid on at the West Somerset Railway for a well-known film director, Richard (Dick) Lester. Dick was visiting the railway with a BBC crew to produce a film that would be televised the following year under the title of *A Comedy Map of Britain*. As the title suggested, this documented the range of locations used across the country in the production of TV and cinema comedies. It was appropriate that Dick Lester should be involved for it was Dick who, 40 years earlier, had directed the Beatles' first film, a comedy entitled *A Hard Day's Night*. The first twenty minutes of that production, which was supposed to reflect a typical day in the life of the Beatles, were filmed at Crowcombe and Minehead stations. And that was how the Minehead branch gained its qualification to feature in *A Comedy Map of Britain*.

BEATLEMANIA

Just over 40 years earlier, in March 1964, a five-carriage, specially-chartered train pulled out of Paddington, bound for the West Country. On board were film director Dick Lester and his crew. With them were actor Wilfred Brambell, already well known for his portrayal of the father of Harold Steptoe in the TV sitcom *Steptoe and Son*, John Runkin, Norman Rossington and Richard Vernon. More significant than all of these were the other passengers, four young lads from Liverpool called John, Paul, George and Ringo. United Artists, the Hollywood film studio, had decided it was time to capitalise on the international popularity of the 'Fab Four'.

The previous year, 'Beatlemania' had entered the dictionary after the Beatles took America by storm following their UK success. An appearance on the Ed Sullivan show had attracted a record-breaking audience of

The Beatles during filming on the Minehead line, 1964.

73 million viewers. By the time they stepped onto the Paddington train, they had already notched up four Number 1 hits in rapid succession and now the peace and tranquillity of West Somerset was about to be shattered. The times and locations for the film shoots were supposed to be secret, but somehow every local teenager, and their teachers, were already aware of them. At Watchet junior school, the teachers were so keen to get a glimpse of the Beatles that they got all the children lined up in the playground and then marched them down to the railway station, where they lined the track. The train rushed through at such a speed that realistically no one could have said who they saw, but they all marched back to school believing they had caught a glimpse of at least one of the famous faces. By now, there were hundreds of screaming fans awaiting their arrival all along the route. Most of them should have been at school, but teachers had been forced to give in to their demands and, in all probability, wanted a piece of the action themselves.

On the Taunton to Minehead line, the train passed through village stations where crowds had gathered to catch a glimpse of the pop stars. At Crowcombe station, it came to a halt while the film crew shot the main film sequences, including one in which Ringo asked a retired colonial-style army officer: 'Hey mister, can we have our ball back?' Over 40 years on, it's the only recollection I have of the whole film other than the music! It was a very thin plot – but better than Cliff Richards' *Summer Holiday*!

Further on, at Minehead station, the four Liverpudlians sat eating a meal in their carriage with hundreds of fans screaming outside their window. Never before had there been such a West Country invasion. Barriers and fences proved no defence against the invading hoards. One teenage girl, having successfully negotiated a barbed wire fence, attempted to cross what appeared to be a wide muddy patch, not realising that after a couple of steps she would be in mud up past her knees. 'Ringo! Save me!' she repeatedly cried, but Ringo was busy eating his meal and it was the local police who dragged her to terra firma.

To control – or tease – the crowds, the carriage curtains were drawn, only to be pulled slightly open now and again for a Beatle face to smile through. With each smile the frenzied females screamed in ecstasy. In due course, the train pulled out and the happy hordes drifted away. The railway gangers, surveying the scene, stood in disbelief as they took in the extent of the damage; broken fences and trampled hedges. In earnest, they set about the repair work but no sooner were they done than the Beatles returned and the whole exercise was repeated.

The national media captured the mood of the moment with headlines such as '500 girls in Beatle Battle' and 'The Beatles go West'. Although this was perhaps the most famous of all the films to take advantage of Somerset's railways, there were many others.

BRANCH LINE FILM FAME

In 1893 the struggling Somerset Coal Canal Company, thanks to the dominance of the railways, was bankrupt. What was left of the business was bought by the Great Western Railway Company who converted the route to railway from Limpley Stoke to Camerton. The line closed in 1951 but therein lay the opportunity, during the following year, for a film company to rent the now disused line to produce a film based on the story of a railway.

The 1953 film *The Titfield Thunderbolt*, now considered an Ealing Film Studio's cinema classic, featured this section of the Somerset & Dorset route over the Cam Brook valley. It tells the story of a group of villagers attempting to prevent the branch line to 'Titfield' being closed. Although the story was inspired by the restoration of the Talyllyn Railway in Wales, the filming was carried out between Camerton and Limpley Stoke, with Monkton Combe station playing the role of Titfield station, and the village of Titfield being portrayed in nearby Freshford. The *Thunderbolt* was in real life the Liverpool & Manchester Railway's *Lion* which, built in 1838, was believed to be the oldest working railway locomotive in the world. Being such an ancient engine, she lacked the power and speed required for the purposes of the film – she was barely capable of reaching 15 mph even when travelling without a load. The solution was simple. To give the appearance of being a much faster train, a former Great Western engine acted as a banker, an engine that pushes a train from the rear, without being connected, and then drops back when no longer required. The banker, pushing from behind, got the *Thunderbolt*'s speed up to 30 mph and then dropped back out of the picture just before the cameras started to roll.

Even earlier than this, in 1931, Camerton station was temporarily renamed Fal Vale for the filming of Arthur Ridley's *The Ghost Train*. For those who have never heard of the author Arthur Ridley, he was in fact the actor who played Private Godfrey in the TV series *Dad's Army*. The filming proved to be a huge attraction with over 5,000 spectators turning up to watch the action. When the film was shown in London, the cinema ticket offices and foyers were decorated in the colours of the Great Western Railway to add to the illusion. The film must have had quite an impact because years later, when the wartime evacuees arrived in the West Country, hundreds of them made their way to Camerton which, thanks to the film, had become a tourist attraction. Six years after the Titfield filming, the nearby Dunkerton Colliery siding was used to film night-time scenes for the Edgar Wallace thriller *Kate Plus Ten*.

In 1962, the pre-knighthood John Betjeman made a BBC documentary *Branch Line Railway*, which was televised the following year and followed the Somerset & Dorset line from Evercreech along its 24-mile stretch to Burnham-on-Sea. The film had a special purpose in that it was Betjeman's unsuccessful appeal to Dr Beeching to spare the line from closure.

CROWCOMBE STATION, STAR OF TV AND CINEMA

Two years later came the Beatles' film and its use of Crowcombe station, a use that turned out to be the first of many. In 1998 *The Land Girls* heavily featured the West Somerset Railway, Crowcombe station in particular, along with Dulverton and Bossington beach. It told the Second World War story of three city women, from contrasting backgrounds, who had all been sent to work on the land, as part of the Land Army, and the strong bond that developed between them. The station also appeared on TV in Southern TV's *Flockton Flyer* and in the 1998 *The Lion, the Witch and the Wardrobe*. When the line reopened in 1976, a former Great Western pannier tank engine, number 6412, was purchased from the Dart Valley Railway and put into service. It was this engine that was to become known to a wide audience of children as the *Flockton Flyer*. Other film productions taking advantage of the West Somerset Railway are *Poirot – The Cornish Mystery* (1989); *Miss Marple – The Mirror Cracked* (1992); *The House of Elliot* (1991–93) and *Allies at War* (2002).

More recently, in September 2006, the line was used in the production of a film that tells the story of Private Sydney Godley, a First World War hero who was awarded the Victoria Cross; released by Channel Five it is entitled *Victoria Cross Heroes*. The film production turned the normally tranquil setting, at the foot of the Quantock Hills, into an apparent battleground awakened by heavy gunfire and explosions. The site of the rail bridge at Bishops Lydeard was turned into the battle-scarred Nimy Bridge on the Conde Canal at Mons in Belgium.

THE EAST SOMERSET RAILWAY

The East Somerset Railway, based at Cranmore, has also provided its services for a catalogue of TV and film productions: the ITV dramas of *Flash Back* starring Graham Stark (1986) and *Maigret* starring Ian Ogilvy (1988); the BBC's *Inside Out* programme about the steam galas at the East and West Somerset Railways (2003); and the film *Hanover Street* starring Harrison Ford and Lesley Anne Down, which features a motorbike chase in which stunt man Eddie Kidd jumps over the cutting near Merryfield Lane!

14

ALL WINDS AND WEATHER

BLIZZARDS

On 30th March 1878 all the rail lines in the county were blocked by snow, but soon reopened using snow ploughs. A far worse blizzard, which swept across the nation in January 1881, resulted in the deaths of hundreds of people and thousands of animals. The night before the blizzard, the temperature had dropped to 18 degrees below freezing. The Taunton to Minehead line was closed for a week, and when a Chard shepherd was frozen to death, it took a team of men five hours to carry his body just one mile. But worse was to come ten years later.

February 1891 had proved to be the lull before the storm. It had been an unseasonably pleasant month and gave no forewarning of the weather ahead. On 9th March, a Monday, heavy snow began to fall in what proved to be a prolonged blizzard. At Burnham-on-Sea, workmen were needed to manually dig out one train, which three engines had failed to rescue. When it eventually reached Highbridge, it stuck fast again and the two engines that were sent to release it became further victims of the same drift. Conditions were particularly bad across the Mendip Hills. At Cannards Grave, the drifts were up to eight or more feet deep, burying one engine so thoroughly that not even its funnel was visible. Across the Somerset & Dorset network, trains were held captive by the snows, which continued unabated for the next two days. In charge of the recovery was Superintendent Dykes. At half past one in the morning, he set out from Bath on a train fitted with a snowplough. They could only get to within four miles of a stranded train and he completed the perilous journey on foot. He had eight engines at the ready at Shepton Mallet. Having assessed the situation, he had four of these coupled together, with a snowplough on the front, and sent them off to clear the line all the way down to the south coast, but not before they spent one and a half hours blasting their way through the Cannards Grave gap. It was late on the following day before they finally reached their destination. To sum it up in so few words fails to do justice to the bravery, stamina and determination of those involved in reopening the lines. Fortunately such winters are few and far between.

FALLING LIKE DOMINOES

During the harsh winter of 1962/63, four engines became entrapped on the line between Bath and Evercreech in what can be described as the domino effect; first one falls, then another. On the Saturday night of 29th December 1962 a snow blizzard created huge drifts. Fortunately there were no trains planned to run on the Sunday, which gave the railway staff a full day to ensure the line was clear. Trains were due to run the following morning, the mail train at 2.40 am, and then freight trains at 3.30 and 5.00 am. During the winter months, a shunting tank engine, number 47557, was kept in readiness with a snowplough fitted back and front, its buffers having been removed. Although hopefully going nowhere, it was kept well maintained, its fire being tended, its water topped up, and ticking over in light steam. That was the theory; however, the very time it was really needed, it had not received the required attention.

Late on that Saturday night, the engine was called into action. When its crew turned up, they found the fire was a mess and the boiler pressure lower than required. They had to start all over again. It was Sunday morning before they could finally get under way to clear the line from Bath to Evercreech. Between Midsomer Norton and Shepton Mallet, the line passed through a gap into which snow had drifted to a considerable depth. The problem for the snowplough was that there was nowhere to push the snow other than from one track onto the other, and so only a single line could be opened through that section. By midnight the plough had finished its work and was returning to Bath for servicing before being connected to the mail train. And so they set off once again, heading south with the snowplough on the front.

During the short time between the plough clearing the line and its return with the mail train, the gap they had recently opened had closed again with drifting snow now having a narrower gap to fill. They struggled over the Masbury summit and past Shepton Mallet but beyond that, as they endeavoured to reach Evercreech, they became trapped in a huge drift and conditions were worsening by the minute.

Meanwhile, the 3.30 am freight train had left Bath and picked up the pilotman at Midsomer Norton. By the time they reached the Masbury summit, which the earlier train had succeeded in negotiating, they found that the conditions had worsened dramatically and they became stuck in a drift. The crew took shelter in a nearby farmhouse while the pilotman trudged his way on foot to Shepton Mallet to report the situation. By then the news had already been transmitted to Bath that the 3.30 had not arrived and so the 5.00 am train was sent out to search for the 3.30. Just like one bad bet following another, the 5.00 am train also got stuck in a drift, and unbeknown to all involved, just yards behind the 3.30. The crew of the 5.00 am train then struggled on foot back over the Masbury summit where, to their relief, they discovered another engine with just a brake van, which had been sent out to rescue them. In the brake van was a crew of twenty men armed with shovels. They too were now stuck in the drift. Four engines had been lost to the elements and the railway company was running out of options. It was by then well into the Monday morning and nothing was moving. Late the following day, clearance operations began in earnest but it was a long and slow process. The 3.30 am train that set out on the Sunday morning of one week finally reached its destination on the Sunday of the following week. It was a further week before the lines in both directions became fully open to traffic.

In the west of Somerset, the Minehead line had also been blocked. Attempts by diesel engines to force their way through proved fruitless and in the end it was good-old-fashioned Victorian steam that was to clear the way, opening up vital links to some of the isolated farms along its length.

The gatecrashers

That same winter, Clarence Rawles was the driver on an engine travelling from Evercreech Junction towards Highbridge. On the footplate were his fireman, Tony Rossiter, and a fellow driver, Ray Sandercock, who was getting a lift home. It was snowing as they passed through Glastonbury but all was going well. Heading towards Ashcott, Driver Rawles looked ahead along the snow-lined track as they approached the curve, around which was the distant signal for the level crossing near Ashcott.

The signal clearly showed the gates as open for the train to pass through and the driver took his engine at full speed towards the gates. As he reached the straight approaching them, he saw the red light on the track indicating that the gates were in fact closed. Unbeknown to him, the weight of snow and ice that had collected on the signal arm was sufficient for it to drop into the down position, incorrectly indicating a clear run ahead. Too late, he shut off the steam and slammed the engine into reverse. The wheels had just started to pick up as the engine careered through the gates, smashing them to smithereens. They finally came to a halt in the goods yards. James Yelling, the guard, climbed down from his van and walked back to the station where he shouted up to the bedroom window of the stationmaster, Archie Atwell. A bleary-eyed Archie peered out through the window, totally unaware of what had just happened to his gates. Seeing the guard below, he told him that he had got fed up waiting for them to arrive and so went to bed. He then suggested that since they knew what to do, they could let themselves through the gates, and he could get back to bed. No problem, was Jimmy's reply as he explained that they'd already done just as he suggested – but he would need to get a new pair of gates.

It appears that Clarence Rawles made a habit of gatecrashing. On another occasion, this time with Alan Mason as his fireman, Clarence left Evercreech at just after six in the morning, taking a goods train to Highbridge. They had passed through West Pennard at a fair rate of knots and were approaching the Pennard Lane crossing. Mr Griggs, who was the gatekeeper, had a reputation for being somewhat tardy in his gate opening operations and trains would often have to wait while he stirred himself to open the line. Clarence, it has to be said, was going too fast, and despite seeing that the crossing light was against him, was unable to stop in time. With the wheels screaming on the track, Rawles turned to his fireman and commented that it was time the gatekeeper was woken up. Out ran the keeper, trousers around his ankles, just in time to see his gates being demolished, with the driver cheerfully bidding him a good morning and pointing out that firewood was now available for collection.

When War Broke Out

Off to the Western Front

The First World War had little impact on Somerset's railways. There were no bombing raids, as in the Second World War, but the railways saw their fair share of wartime traffic. Troops in the Great War were generally based in locally recruited regiments, such as the Somerset Light Infantry. The effects of this policy could be quite devastating when regiments were almost wiped out on the Western Front, with many villages losing all their menfolk because they all signed up together. Nonetheless, they were proud to go and would leave en masse by train from their local stations, friends and family crowding the platforms to wave their farewells, never knowing how many would return. Somerset, in a way, was luckier than other counties. It suffered losses as much as anywhere else but somehow not with such impact on small communities.

Troops destined for the Western Front line up at Bridgwater station, 1914.

The other role for the railways was in carrying the thousands of horses required to go overseas and these were gathered at railway marshalling yards, in particular at Yeovil, Taunton and Bridgwater.

Evacuees by the Trainload

In September 1939 cheap day excursions came to an abrupt end with the outbreak of war. The nation heard the Prime Minister's words, 'This country is at war with

Germany', over their wireless sets. Trips to Burnham, Exeter and Exmouth were cancelled. Gone were the trainloads of smiling faces with buckets and spades, to be replaced with the sad, tired, confused and frightened faces of those thousands of children evacuated from London's East End to the relative safety of the West Country. Gas masks were distributed, to be carried at all times. The local papers printed an article about the King's speech and on the need for 'Somerset homes for mothers and children'. As the men of the county were called up and headed away, evacuees from London began to arrive. Across the nation, three million women and children were on the move. In the Yeovil area alone, 11,000 arrived on the evacuee trains, 4,400 being allocated to the borough of Yeovil. Bridgwater took nearly 6,500, over a thousand in the first week to be housed in the town with a further thousand for the villages, those from the East End of London arriving first.

It was tough on the children as they arrived at railway stations, bewildered and afraid, with luggage labels giving their identity tied to their lapels. In many cases, brothers and sisters were separated. Scabies, ringworm and other complaints were amongst the problems they brought to the county.

Parents were free to visit their children whenever they could – but it was very difficult with London being bombed and travel restricted. When they arrived, it got no better. In case of a German invasion, all place names and direction signs had been removed and the East Enders found it daunting to try and locate the villages. The evacuation continued throughout the rest of the year and was still running at the rate of thousands per month through to the summer of the following year.

PILL BOXES AND DAD'S ARMY

During the Second World War the railway system provided a vital aspect of the communications network. It was the principal method of transporting troops and munitions, and was a prime target for enemy bombing, so naturally it had to be protected at all costs. To defend the network, a system of pill boxes was constructed at strategic points along the tracks, as well as along canals and roads. In fact there was a defensive line of pill boxes and anti-tank obstacles from Weston-super-Mare, along the coast down to Burnham-on-Sea, down through Bridgwater and Chard, and all the way down to Seaton on the Devon coast. Part of the purpose of this line, which followed the railway and canals for most of its route, was to cut off the south-west of England in the case of a German invasion on the West Country beaches. Cornwall, Devon and a large part of Somerset would be sacrificed in order to protect London and the industrial Midlands. A further similar line ran from Burnham-on-Sea along the line of the old S&D through Wells and Radstock to just south of Bath and then down to Frome. But there was no point in having these defensive positions without the military force to defend them, and hence the Home Guard was formed, or 'Dad's Army' as we popularly know it today.

The Home Guard, or Land Defence Volunteers, was set up in May 1940 to protect the local area from enemy invaders. Bridgwater had its own unit, the 10th Somerset Battalion under the command of Lieutenant-Colonel R. Chamberlain, based at the Drill Hall and manned by 2,500 men split into platoons. Number 6 platoon was reserved for railwaymen, with a particular requirement to defend the Somerset Bridge rail crossing over the River Parrett. Initially they were only armed with pick-axe handles and an armband labelled 'LDV'. Then Lord Wharton from Goathurst supplied them with a couple of double-barrelled shotguns; however, within a week one had been dropped and broken. Eventually uniforms, arms and other kit arrived and the LDV looked a more serious unit. Three years later, they even had grenades and there was many a Somerset home where a rifle stood in the corner of the front room.

Bridgwater's Number 6 platoon drilled regularly in the grounds of Eastover School, next to the railway lines. On an exercise in which they combined with the contingent from the local Cellophane factory, a misdirected smoke grenade brought a straight-through passenger train to an unexpected stop.

At the back of the railway station was a spigot mortar gun emplacement. On an exercise with a Scottish regiment, who were conveniently in the area, a thunder-flash was lobbed into the emplacement and set fire to the seat of the trousers of an LDV railwayman, who promptly resigned. The Scots also managed to blow out several windows in Devonshire Street and a freshly-painted house had to be redecorated.

Taunton's 'A' and 'C' companies defended the railway tunnel at Whiteball, near Wellington, and an old rail coach was kept in situ to be used as a guardroom. On one occasion the telephone wires that connected them with the Home Guard units across the county border in Devon were cut. This act of sabotage coincided with the escape of a convict from Dartmoor prison, which may account for the incident.

UNDER ATTACK

In the Yeovil district, the principal unit was the 22nd Devon (5th Southern Railway) Battalion. 'A' company was based in Yeovil and both 'A' and 'B' companies consisted of men from Chard Junction and Yeovil stations, with Somerset & Dorset men being members of 'E' company at Templecombe. Yeovil, with its rail junction, the Westland's factory and Yeovilton air base, was a prime target for German bombers. The first raid came in September 1940 when 50 German bombers were repelled by British fighters, dropping their 300 bombs instead on Sherborne.

In December 1940 the War Department constructed an ammunition depot at Dimmer to the west of Castle Cary and a fan of additional railway sidings was installed. This made Castle Cary a prime target and almost two years later, in September 1942, the area suffered its first fatal attack. Engine number 1729, a saddle tank shunter, had left its Yeovil shed to help a freight train up the Brewham Bank and then returned to Castle Cary where there was a change of crew. Jack Rogers, the driver, and Tom Whittle, the fireman, took over the controls and were shunting carriages to create a train to go to Durston. Their engine stood ready to enter the goods yard. Then, from out of the blue, a German Junkers 88 bomber flew in low along the Weymouth line, beneath the radar level, and dropped four bombs.

The first 250 kg bomb found its target, a direct hit on engine 1729. It came to rest buried in the track ballast right beneath the engine's driving wheel, where it lay unseen beneath the footplate of the engine. The driver and fireman, curious to know where it was, leaned over the side of the cab to see the bomb immediately beneath them. It had failed to explode. Both men instinctively turned to run, but the bomb had a delayed action timer and it exploded. Rogers, the driver, was blown out of his cab and killed. Whittle had just moved clear of the covered section of the half cab and believes that he was blown clear and hence survived, but with injuries. When he came to, he was lying in a crater, naked apart from one shoe, the pocket of his trousers hanging from his trouser belt and one shoulder of his jacket. Eight of the wagons were wrecked with five others badly damaged. Several telegraph poles were brought down and the crater in which Tom Whittle found himself was 12 feet across and over 4 feet deep.

The parcel office, goods shed and signal box were destroyed by the second bomb, with the signalman, Arthur Sibley, being killed in the action. An even bigger crater of 22 feet across and 6 deep remained where the signal box once stood. Next to be destroyed was the Railway Hotel, the bomb bouncing through the front wall, knocking out the back wall as it exploded, and simultaneously damaging the nearby Prideaux' dairy and a row of three cottages, whilst the final bomb landed harmlessly in the River Brue. All bombs having been released, the German turned his plane for another run, this time strafing the railway with machine-gun fire. Two more railwaymen lost their lives.

By 9.15 am it was all over. With Castle Cary being an important junction, it was vital to get the network back up and running. Railway staff rallied around and by 11 am some trains were running, with normal service being resumed within a few days. The incident had highlighted the need to have plans in place for alternative routes should such an attack occur again, and the need to spread the storage of engines across different sites to reduce the potential for high losses in the event of a raid.

On 5th September, two nights after the attack on Castle Cary, it was Templecombe's turn. Another Junkers 88 attacked, dropping four heavy bombs. The Somerset & Dorset line was hit, and knocked out of action, just as the Bath train was pulling out of the station. The windows of its guard's van were taken out by the blast. The train's fireman mistakenly commented that the detonators, which are placed on a track to warn drivers of problems on the line, were particularly loud – only to be told that the sound he had heard was bombing! The Southern Railway took a hit close to the parcels office where a wheeltapper, a ganger, a greaser and the head porter were all killed. One of the dead men was found still upright, his backbone pinned to the wall. Although the rail network was the real target, there was considerable damage to the civilian areas. Two churches, two hotels and scores of houses were damaged. Thirteen people were killed and seventeen injured.

Not all deaths on the rail system were caused by enemy attacks. In one sad incident, a Polish pilot, who was part of 313 Squadron based at Churchstanton, was practising a mock attack on a train. Somehow he lost control and flew his Spitfire straight into the second carriage of a Great Western train at Hillfarrance, killing himself and injuring a woman passenger.

THE GIS ARRIVE

In 1942 the American forces joined the effort to restore peace in Europe. They arrived in their hundreds of thousands. It was from the West Country that the Americans would embark for the D-Day landings, hence a high concentration of their forces in this part of the world. One legacy from that period was the Musgrove Park Hospital in Taunton, which was built to take the American wounded. The GIs were very popular with the Somerset children (chocolate bars and chewing gum) and the womenfolk (cigarettes and nylon stockings), but not so popular with the men (overpaid, over-sexed and over here!). However, my wife's grandfather, who was a Great Western engine driver based at Taunton at the time, told me how he changed his attitude towards the Americans when he was involved in bringing trainloads of their wounded back to Musgrove for treatment.

On more than one occasion during the war, very important passengers were to pass through Yeovil station. At a quarter to midnight on 12th August 1943, General Eisenhower arrived in his private train, codenamed 'Alive', consisting of seven carriages plus two vans holding his six motor cars. In mid-January 1944, it stopped overnight at Chard Junction. In those months leading up to the D-Day landings, the military traffic increased significantly. Enormous volumes of ammunition and the equipment of war were being stored in readiness for their final deployment. British and American troops handling ammunition at Marston Magna alone amounted to several hundred. In the two days before D-Day, the entire stock disappeared, on its way to Normandy, and not a soldier remained. At the same time, the movement of troop trains towards the coast was relentless, to be followed days later by the movement in the opposite direction of hospital trains, fortunately not in such high numbers as had been planned for. Next came the trainloads of German prisoners of war.

One incident that occurred during all that movement came near Henstridge. Since this was wartime, and the incident involved the military, much of the detail, including the total number of deaths, was never officially released. It was March 1944; a double-headed train carrying troops was passing under the A30 trunk road when an American tank transporter was crossing the bridge under which the train was travelling. The access to the bridge was narrow and the driver managed to collide with its parapet. The bridge then collapsed under the weight, leaving the transporter and tank tumbling down the bank onto the train below. Its timing was tragically perfect, landing smack between the two engines, severing their coupling link. The leading engine stayed upright as it headed down the track with wreckage strewn across it. It took some while for the driver to bring it to a halt, but not before he had passed through Henstridge. At the station, William Jackson, a porter, was doing some maintenance work to an oil signal lamp at the top of a signal post when it was struck by the passing debris. Down came the post, with William clinging to its top. It was a lucky escape as he landed unhurt by the experience.

The second engine took the bulk of the huge weight of the descending load, its cab being completely crushed. Despite the heavy load by which it had just been hit, it still had sufficient momentum to continue, but now off the rails and heading into a field where it finished up on its side. Harold Burford, the driver, and his fireman managed to put out the fire in their engine's boiler and saw to the wounded passengers. Harold was perhaps in too severe a state of shock to realise that the back of his clothing was smouldering. Whilst he was tending the wounded, someone else was putting out his personal fire. Of the six carriages in the train, five were wrecked and at least six soldiers killed, although the total numbers have never been released.

BATH BLITZ

In April 1942 there was devastating bombing of the city of Bath and most of the roof of Bath's Green Park station was destroyed. The fear of further raids was heightened when sparks from passing engines set fire to the dry grass verges beside the tracks. Night after night, through the dry spells, residents would rush out in the darkness to extinguish the fires that otherwise might have attracted the German bombers like moths to a candle. On the positive side, the rail tunnel at Combe Down, the site of previous disasters, at least offered unofficial shelter during the bombing raids when nearby residents would take refuge in the niches within the tunnel wall. Engine drivers would often see their frightened faces in the glow from the engine.

UNEQUAL PAY

With so many men away in the armed forces, it was necessary for women to take on what would normally have been male roles. Where the rail network was concerned, with troops and armaments on the move, this was critical to the war effort. At Minehead station, as elsewhere, ticket sales became the role of the ladies, although they were not paid as much as a man doing the equivalent work. Minehead, once 1942 had arrived, saw large numbers of American and Canadian troops, many of them being billeted at Dunster. Minehead's North Hill was used as one of their training grounds, their tanks being brought by train into the goods yard at Minehead.

The hours of working could be long, with a 7 o'clock morning start, and the last train due in at half past ten in the evening. The timing of this last train could be quite unpredictable. If there had been heavy bombing in London, then the trains leaving the city could be delayed by hours. This rippled all the way across the network, with connecting trains having to wait. So the last train of the evening could quite often arrive in the early hours of the following morning. Being wartime, there was no overtime payment but the senior staff appreciated the ladies' efforts. Now and again, once the station had been locked up, and if the pubs were still open, one of the senior staff would take them for a well-earned drink in the Beach Hotel. This turned into an embarrassing arrangement on one occasion when, having secured the station, and with the ladies and their supervisor supping their drinks, a train, which somehow they had overlooked, arrived at the station. Their first awareness of this was when the train's guard tapped on the pub window asking them if they were going to unlock the station or should he get all the passengers to climb over the fence?

16

YOU HAD TO LAUGH

Sometimes humorous incidents occur that, on their own, lack sufficient material to justify their own chapter. One example is the case of a railway policeman seen running into a signal box in pursuit of a runaway hound, shouting: 'Stop that dog. He's a parcel!' Nonetheless, such tales are well worth the telling and can justify their own pages when gathered together.

HAVE YOU GOT A LIGHT, BOY?

It was during the days of steam that heavily-loaded freight trains would struggle to make their way up the Wellington bank, a steep hill between Wellington and the Whiteball tunnel. To cater for such occasions, a tank engine was kept in a siding at Wellington station to provide the extra power required to complete the ascent. A blast on the whistle from the driver of the freight train was all that was required as a signal for the tank engine crew to swing into action.

Their technique was to gently approach the freight train from the rear, touching bumpers in a controlled fashion as they made contact. The freight train could then take full advantage of the extra shove from behind and complete its journey up the ascent. The shunting engine was never connected to the main train, it just gently pushed and then simply applied its brakes and returned in reverse once its involvement was complete.

It was on one such occasion, in the dark of night, that the crew of the shunter left their siding and approached the slow-moving freight train. The driver on the right-hand side peered cautiously into the darkness, carefully judging his speed and the rate at which the gap was closing between themselves and the rear light of the freight train. On his left, his fireman was stoking as the engine steamed forward. The fireman, satisfied that the fire was burning well, looked to his driver to check that all was OK. It was just the two of them in the cab, in almost total darkness, just the dim light from the fire and their cab lamp; two men on a slow moving train, not another soul anywhere around. So imagine the terror that was struck into the heart of the fireman when he felt a cold, clammy hand grasp his shoulder from behind. In horror he let out a scream, terrified as to what kind of night-born creature had claimed him for whatever purpose. The purpose, however, was soon revealed as a voice from behind enquired, 'Have you got a light, boy?'

It was the guard from the train they had been assisting. With the tank engine in direct contact with the brake van, the guard, who had cigarettes but no matches, simply stepped from his van onto the plate at the front of the tank engine, made his way down its side and into the cab entrance, just as the fireman had turned his back. The timing was perfect, the impact immediate and terrifying, and created one of those simple moments that provide a tale which never enters the railway record books but gets passed down through oral legend for generations to come.

You go your way, and I'll go mine

Much can be written about runaway trains but, generally speaking, the engine and the wagons all go together. Once in a blue moon, the unexpected happens and a train goes off in two directions at the same time. It was 1958 and the afternoon milk train was on its way from Highbridge to Templecombe. This involved passing West Pennard and ascending the steep incline of Pylle bank. The engine was working hard as it made its slow uphill progress, belching smoke, with bright-red sparks showering out from her chimney. But suddenly, shortly after passing a crossing, the load got lighter, a coupling pin had sheared. Whilst the front end of the train now made better speed up the bank, the back-half of the train began its descent back towards West Pennard.

The crossing keeper, realising what had happened, notified the signalman down the line, who in turn set the line to direct the runaway carriages into a siding. By now travelling at high speed, the runaway section safely negotiated the points and ran on until crashing into the stop blocks. Wagons lay scattered across the field. The brake van mercifully stayed upright and from it emerged the guard who staggered across the field in a state of total confusion.

A local farmer saw the train passing his farm, one section going one way, the rest the other. He jumped into his Morris Minor pick-up and headed to where the crashed wagons had come to rest. Other farmers had already arrived. Milk was seeping into the ground and large rolls of barbed wire were tangled up together. When the signalman arrived and saw the damage, he reflected on the appropriate adage that there is no use crying over spilt milk – nor tangled barbed wire. And so he gave the farmers the nod; they could help themselves to the wire. The site was cleared in a flash, the farmers going away with about 20 rolls apiece. Every cloud has a silver lining.

THE BUCKET

Back in the days of steam, there were far more train services running than we witness today. Many of these were very local in nature, such as 'The Bucket', which ran between Castle Cary and Taunton, stopping at all stations. It was inevitably a slow service and one that had to take a side-line now and again to let the faster trains through.

This then brings us to the name 'The Bucket', an unusual title that was never officially endorsed by the railway company, but was how the slow, stop-at-every-station service was popularly known. The apparent explanation goes as follows. When the faster, non-stop train was due, the slow, local train would be placed on the loop line and there its crew would wait patiently for the signal to change, letting it proceed on its journey. As long as the signal arm was raised, ie horizontal, they had to wait. When it was lowered, they could proceed. These delays were often protracted and frequently long enough to take a reasonable nap. And so one of the crew would scale the signal gantry and place a bucket on the arm of the signal where it would silently swing in the breeze until the signalman lowered the arm, giving the 'Clear to proceed'. The bucket would then fall off the arm, hitting the ground with a resounding crash, awakening the slumbering crew. The simplest ideas are always the best!

THE FISH AND CHIP SPECIAL

If 'The Bucket' is an unusual name, perhaps 'The Fish and Chip Special' has a more obvious origin. For many years, the last passenger train leaving Bath's Green Park station was usually around 9 o'clock at night. During the 1930s a late night special was laid on twice a week, the mid-week one being on Wednesday, market day, and the weekend special on the Saturday night. These late night specials would leave Bath at around 11 o'clock. This was a convenient time for the young lads from Wellow, Shoscombe, Radstock and Midsomer Norton who would spend an evening in Bath, perhaps with a girl at the cinema, followed by a few beers. Whereas today's young drinkers would pick up a kebab on the way home, in the 1930s it was fish and chips, just in time to catch the last train. By the time the revellers had left the train and headed for their beds, the carriages were littered with the left-over wrappers, hence the title of 'The Fish and Chip Special'.

Apart from the litter, other problems were the occasional unconscious drunks. They would often just manage to board the train, but then pass out before reaching their ultimate destination. Usually there was someone to put them off at the right station. However, on one occasion, a passenger was unconscious before even boarding the train. The platform staff, on checking his pockets, found a return ticket for Radstock. They lifted him onto a wheeled trolley, trucked him to the train and put him in the guard's van. At Radstock, he was offloaded, just like a piece of luggage.

IT'S ENOUGH TO MAKE A VICAR SWEAR

It was one of my mother's favourite expressions. She never swore herself – but when circumstances would have caused lesser mortals to blaspheme, she would simply say, 'It's enough to make a vicar swear!' Of course, they never do – or do they?

It was during the war years and in the blackout. The late-night passenger train arrived at Wells and, in the total darkness, the engine driver found it difficult to judge the exact position of the platform. As a consequence, he overran by about the length of three carriages. In itself, it wasn't that serious, most of his passengers would still get off on the right platform. On board was a vicar, on his way to the cathedral at Wells. Stepping off the train, he safely alighted on the platform, but he was not where he thought he would be. Past experience had shown him that if he walked forward, he would be heading straight for the exit, or at least the walls of the platform buildings. Sadly for our vicar, he was much further along the platform than he could possibly have imagined. Now at this point it is worth explaining the way that cattle are handled at rail stations. To board cattle on a train, they clearly need to be on a raised platform, level with the cattle wagons. When they arrive at the station, they are off-loaded into a marshalling yard and then driven up a sloping ramp into the cattle pens, pending their boarding onto the train. Cattle, however, have never learnt how to use the 'facilities' and hence leave their dung wherever it suits them. The dung from the pens is then washed or shovelled off into a slurry trap ready for removal.

Back to our vicar and you are probably already ahead of me. Misplaced on the platform, and heading straight across it, in the total darkness he plummeted into the slurry pit. Several minutes later, with blood pouring from a cut on his forehead and covered from head to foot in cows' muck, he finally made his way through the booking office door to confront the station staff, who stared at him in total disbelief. Never lost for words, he declared, 'I've just fallen down a bloody great hole!' Enough to make a vicar swear, indeed.

THOSE UNGUARDED MOMENTS

In the 1950s, when the S&D still had a service running from Bridgwater, the old Bridgwater North station was just a matter of yards from the Cross Rifles public house. This was a favourite with the railmen of the Somerset & Dorset. It was one guard's habit, whilst the goods were being loaded by a porter, to pop down to the Cross Rifles and have a couple of pints before it was time to pull out. One chilly October evening, when there was a cold dampness in the air, the fireman and driver were preparing the engine. They had good pressure and were ready to move. The steam from the engine lingered in an unmoving cloud, along the length of the station platform, enshrouding the train in a ghostly mist.

The young porter was new to the job and keen to impress. Having loaded the goods van in double-quick time, he closed its doors. The driver leaned out of his cabin and peered back, through the mist, to the rear of the train, looking for the all clear signal from the guard. Seeing a figure in the right position, he waved. The keen-to-please porter, not wanting to cause offence, waved back. The driver, believing it to be his guard signalling, put the engine into forward gear, opened the regulator, and gently pulled away. Back at the Cross Rifles, the guard had just finished his second pint and was putting on his jacket when he heard his train leaving without him!

In a similar story from Minehead, and from the same period, an extrovert rail enthusiast was patrolling Minehead station, spotter's guide in hand, wearing a railway worker's hat, and sporting a flag and whistle. Deep into his role-playing fantasy, he blew his whistle, waved his flag and was delighted when the driver responded and took the train out of the station with its guard still finishing off a cup of tea in the parcel office.

But perhaps the most amusing tale of an unguarded moment comes from the pre-war years on the Cheddar Valley branch of the Great Western Railway. The GWR staff had been 'blessed' with an over-enthusiastic guard. He was full of arrogant, self-centred flamboyance. He loved to be the centre of attention and, as a guard, the opportunities were plentiful. At each station, when the time came to pull out, he would step onto the platform and flourish his guard's flag with intense energy, showmanship and flair – and this was directly proportional to the number of people observing his performance.

On one occasion, having pulled in at a station, he realised that a railway inspector was on the platform talking to the stationmaster. These were people to impress. It was an opportunity he was not prepared to miss. Leaving his guard's van, he paraded up and down the platform, checking the state of all the carriages, pompously ensuring that he was being observed by the two senior gentlemen. He was so irritating! Driver, fireman, platform staff, linesmen were unanimous in their aggravation. A plot was hatched.

With the driver's approval, one of the linesmen sneaked along the length of the train on the blind side, unseen by the guard. Having reached the brake van, he uncoupled it from the rest of the train. When the time came to leave, the guard, by now in his van, stepped back onto the platform with even greater flamboyance than usual, and with the stationmaster and inspector keenly watching, he flourished his flag and blew his whistle as never before. Proud of his performance, delighted at having been observed by two such important gentlemen, he stepped back into the brake van and watched in shame and embarrassment as the train pulled out whilst he remained unmoved, apart from a deepening red face. Such moments are to be cherished, long remembered and still written about decades later.

THE RAILWAY'S INSPECTOR CLOUSEAU

I remember when my father was a 'Postman Higher Grade', a role in which he was responsible for ensuring that all the registered mail was kept secure in a metal caged area. Somehow registered packages were disappearing and no one quite knew where. It was between Taunton and Bridgwater. Postal and rail staff fell equally under suspicion, including my father, who of course resented this. The problem was finally resolved and the culprit brought to book. The suspicion was lifted from those like my father but it left a bad taste, a feeling that his years of loyal service had counted for nothing when the chips were down. This was during the early 1950s, when I was a young child but nonetheless was aware of the tension at home. It was in later years that I was to discover how the case was solved.

It was not only registered parcels that were disappearing; it was boxes of cigarettes as well. During those days, high volumes of commercial goods were delivered by rail. When goods went missing, they could have been lifted by anyone along the chain. With valuable items such as registered mail, which often contained money, and tobacco products involved, an investigation was required. The epicentre of the thefts appeared to be Taunton.

A Taunton-based railway policeman went undercover, actually literally under the covers. He would hide himself in a specially-adapted large laundry basket. These baskets conveniently were part of the regular deliveries on that particular line. Obviously it's very difficult to mount such an operation in total secrecy. Inevitably staff at the station where he was loaded onto the train knew of his presence and his purpose. Trip after trip, from his hiding place, he observed the activity as the train stopped at the various stations. As the days passed, he became more of a joke and gradually the word leaked out until even the engine drivers and their guards knew what he was doing.

The laundry baskets were supported on a set of four wheels, to make them easy to manoeuvre. This gave the guard the opportunity to ensure that the 'observation' basket was placed centrally in the carriage, giving it greater freedom of movement. The driver's role was then to give the unsuspecting policeman a bumpy ride, deliberately causing the goods van to jerk as it started, and then jerk again as it reached the limit of its links. The basket shot like a pinball, first one way, then the next, and this happened at every station. Hopefully the policeman thought it was worth the effort when the culprit was finally apprehended.

In another example of a driver-generated prank, a porter from Wellington station was the deserving victim. He had focused his attention on the more-generous first-class passengers in order to acquire more than his fair share of tips. He was so persistently first in line, that his colleagues felt it time to teach him a lesson. So one day when he boarded a train with a passenger's baggage, as he was loading it into the luggage racks, the carriage door was closed by a fellow porter. The guard waved his flag and out went the train with the annoying porter stranded on board. Pulling down the window, he leaned out and called for someone to stop the train. 'Don't worry,' was the response, 'we'll get the signalman to stop the train and let you off. You can catch the next goods train back!'

Unbeknown to the porter, further plans had already been arranged. The signalman, as promised, stopped the train and allowed him to get off and also, as promised, the next goods train was similarly stopped so that he could get on the footplate and return to the station. What he didn't expect was what was about to unfold. The train rapidly increased in speed to 70 mph and rocketed through the Whiteball tunnel. The porter was terrified as the engine rocked from side to side but matters were about to get worse. The driver collapsed onto the footplate, struck down by an apparent heart attack. The porter watched in disbelief as the fireman appeared to do nothing. 'Stop the train! Stop the train!' yelled the porter. 'Don't know how!' said the fireman. 'I ain't bin tawt yet! I only joined last week. I'm getting out of here,' and he stepped to the edge of the footplate ready to leap to safety.

It was only when the porter himself was seen to be about to do the same that the two characters revealed their secret. The lesson had been learned – work as a team or don't work with us.

TALES OF SOMERSET STEAM

TRAIN STOP AT THE CHARD ROAD HOTEL!

In 1863 a branch line was opened to Chard from the London & South Western Railway's main line to Exeter. A section of that line between Chard and Chard Junction runs downhill at a 1 in 80 gradient. This once proved too much for an engine and its two carriages in the 1930s. It was unable to stop at the end of the line, ran over the buffers and finished up parked in the middle of the road. Twenty years later, another driver had to go one better. His engine was hauling three carriages and he wanted to get the engine to the other end of the train. What he did next was common, but not good, practice. He pulled the carriages onto the gentle downhill approach to a set of points leading into a siding. He then uncoupled the engine and ran it into the siding. While this was happening, the carriages very slowly began to roll downhill towards the points. The driver's next job was to run back, switch the points to keep the carriages on the main line, rather than follow the engine into the siding, and then, once they were past the points, he would leap into the brake van and apply the brake. He could then go back to the siding to bring out the engine, now at the other end of the train.

He had done this countless times before but this time it all went wrong. He was just about to step up onto the brake van when he slipped and fell over. The carriages were now gaining their own momentum and as he ran to leap aboard, he could only watch as they accelerated away from him, heading downhill towards Chard Junction. They were doing about 40 mph when they hit and demolished a set of buffers, passed through a fence, safely crossed the road and came to a final halt in the car park of the Chard Road Hotel.

INDEX

Index